Bipolar
Disorders

Diseases and Disorders

ReferencePoint
Press™

San Diego, CA

Other books in the Compact Research series include:

Current Issues

Abortion

Assisted Suicide

Biomedical Ethics

Civil Rights

Cloning

The Death Penalty

Energy Alternatives

Free Speech

Gay Rights

Health Care

Human Rights

Global Warming and
   Climate Change

Gun Control

Illegal Immigration

Islam

National Security

Nuclear Weapons and
   Security

Obesity

School Violence

Stem Cells

Terrorist Attacks

U.S. Border Control

Video Games

World Energy Crisis

Diseases and Disorders

ADHD

Alzheimer's Disease

Anorexia

Autism

Down Syndrome

Hepatitis

HPV

Meningitis

Phobias

Sexually Transmitted
   Diseases

Drugs

Alcohol

Club Drugs

Cocaine and Crack

Hallucinogens

Heroin

Inhalants

Marijuana

Methamphetamine

Nicotine and Tobacco

Performance-Enhancing
   Drugs

Prescription Drugs

Steroids

Bipolar Disorders

by Hal Marcovitz

Diseases and Disorders

ReferencePoint
Press™

San Diego, CA

For more information, contact:
ReferencePoint Press, Inc.
PO Box 27779
San Diego, CA 92198
www. ReferencePointPress.com

LIBRARY OF CONGRESS CATALOGING-IN-PUBLICATION DATA

Bipolar disorders / by Hal Marcovitz.
    p. cm. — (Compact research)
  Includes bibliographical references and index.
  ISBN-13: 978-1-60152-066-1 (hardback)
  ISBN-10: 1-60152-066-2 (hardback)
  1. Manic-depressive illness—Popular works.
  RC516.M375 2008
  616.89'5—dc22
                                                 2008037721

Contents

Foreword

66Where is the knowledge we have lost in information?99

—T.S. Eliot, "The Rock."

As modern civilization continues to evolve, its ability to create, store, distribute, and access information expands exponentially. The explosion of information from all media continues to increase at a phenomenal rate. By 2020 some experts predict the worldwide information base will double every 73 days. While access to diverse sources of information and perspectives is paramount to any democratic society, information alone cannot help people gain knowledge and understanding. Information must be organized and presented clearly and succinctly in order to be understood. The challenge in the digital age becomes not the creation of information, but how best to sort, organize, enhance, and present information.

ReferencePoint Press developed the *Compact Research* series with this challenge of the information age in mind. More than any other subject area today, researching current issues can yield vast, diverse, and unqualified information that can be intimidating and overwhelming for even the most advanced and motivated researcher. The *Compact Research* series offers a compact, relevant, intelligent, and conveniently organized collection of information covering a variety of current topics ranging from illegal immigration and methamphetamine to diseases such as anorexia and meningitis.

The series focuses on three types of information: objective single-author narratives, opinion-based primary source quotations, and facts and statistics. The clearly written objective narratives provide context and reliable background information. Primary source quotes are carefully selected and cited, exposing the reader to differing points of view. And facts and statistics sections aid the reader in evaluating perspectives. Presenting these key types of information creates a richer, more balanced learning experience.

For better understanding and convenience, the series enhances information by organizing it into narrower topics and adding design features that make it easy for a reader to identify desired content. For example, in *Compact Research: Illegal Immigration*, a chapter covering the economic impact of illegal immigration has an objective narrative explaining the various ways the economy is impacted, a balanced section of numerous primary source quotes on the topic, followed by facts and full-color illustrations to encourage evaluation of contrasting perspectives.

The ancient Roman philosopher Lucius Annaeus Seneca wrote, "It is quality rather than quantity that matters." More than just a collection of content, the *Compact Research* series is simply committed to creating, finding, organizing, and presenting the most relevant and appropriate amount of information on a current topic in a user-friendly style that invites, intrigues, and fosters understanding.

Bipolar Disorders at a Glance

What Are Bipolar Disorders?

Bipolar disorders are mental illnesses that manifest themselves in wild mood swings, ranging from intense euphoria to deep depression. They are unpredictable and can endure for days, weeks, or months.

Three Main Types of Bipolar Disorders

There are three main categories of bipolar disorders. People with the most common form, bipolar I, experience severe mood swings. People with bipolar II and hypomania undergo long periods of depression interrupted by brief periods of a lesser form of mania. In the third type, cyclothymic disorder, people experience minor mood swings that still affect their quality of life.

Who Is Bipolar?

An estimated 5.7 million Americans are bipolar, but the number could be much higher because psychiatrists often misdiagnose the illness as depression. Moreover, mental health professionals are convinced that an estimated million or more children could be suffering from undiagnosed bipolar disorder.

What Causes Bipolar Disorders?

Mental health professionals suspect many causes, including chemical imbalances in the brain, inherited traits from parents, and cultural and social factors.

How Are Bipolar Disorders Diagnosed?

Patients typically seek a doctor's help during a period of depression; after questioning the patient, the doctor will learn of manic episodes as well. Also, the doctor will question the patient about a family history of bipolar disorder.

Main Symptoms

In the manic phase, symptoms include intense euphoria, irritability, excessive talking, egotistical feelings, little need for sleep, promiscuity, and desire to spend money. In the depressive phase, symptoms include overwhelming sadness, fatigue, change in appetite, and pessimism.

Further Complications

Bipolar patients are susceptible to hypothyroidism, in which the body's metabolism slows and does not burn calories at a normal rate.

Severe Consequences

As many as 80 percent of bipolar patients abuse alcohol and drugs. They are also heavy smokers, which can lead to lung diseases. Bipolar patients are also at high risk of committing suicide; as many as 15 percent of bipolar patients take their own lives.

Treatment

The drug lithium is able to control symptoms in most bipolar patients, although doctors sometimes supplement lithium with other drugs to help control the depressive episodes. Psychotherapy is also regarded as an important component of a bipolar patient's treatment.

Research Continues

Scientists are working on a connection between genes and bipolar patients. If genes can be identified and tests developed to pinpoint bipolar disorder, it can be diagnosed earlier.

Overview

66 **Manic depression is not a safe ride. It doesn't go from point A to point B in a familiar, friendly pattern. It's chaotic, unpredictable. You never know where you're heading next.** 99

—Terri Cheney, a bipolar patient and author of *Manic: A Memoir.*

What Are Bipolar Disorders and What Are the Symptoms?

Bipolar disorder, also known as manic depression, is a mental illness characterized by dramatic mood swings that range from extreme euphoria to deep depression. In the stage known as mania, patients are often unstable and reckless. In the depressive stage, they may not be able to summon the energy to get out of bed.

Bipolar episodes can last for days, weeks, or months. Bipolar patients may feel fine and able to function normally for extended periods but suddenly and without warning their moods may change. In the manic stage, they may become giddy and talkative. They may make impulsive decisions and engage in risky behavior. Or they may become depressed—sullen and anxious, often entertaining thoughts of suicide.

British comedian Stephen Fry wrestled with his mood swings for years without knowing what was wrong. At one low point in his life, he found himself sitting in his garage with the door closed, trying to decide whether to turn on his car's ignition and take his own life. He finally shook himself out of his depression and went to see a doctor, who told him he is bipolar. Said Fry, "For the first time, at the age of 37, I had a diagnosis that explained the massive highs and miserable lows I'd lived with all my life."[1]

According to the National Institute of Mental Health, about 2.6 percent of the American population over the age of 18, or about 5.7 million people, are believed to suffer from bipolar disorders to some degree. Experts suspect the number could be higher because many people have not been diagnosed. Men and women are afflicted by bipolar disorders equally.

Common Symptoms

The wild and erratic mood swings are the most pronounced symptoms of bipolar disorders. In the manic phase, typical symptoms include intense euphoria but also irritability, excessive talking, a desire to move quickly on ideas, thoughtlessness, and egotistical feelings. Marisa Robbins, the wife of former professional football player Barret Robbins, recalled her husband's wild and erratic behavior during his manic episodes:

> He would talk a little faster. Some of his ideas were faster and he would even drive faster. He'd start listening to his louder, hard-core rap music. As it progressed, I could actually see a difference in his body language. He sometimes got fidgety and would have these rapid movements with his hands. He started spending more, wanting to put $7,000 in a sound system and a TV in his Mercedes.[2]

In bipolar disorders, the manic phase is frequently followed by a depressive phase. Common symptoms of the depressive phase may include intense sadness as well as fatigue, insomnia, changes in appetite, agitation, pessimism, and thoughts of suicide. Robbins experienced those symptoms as well. Says his wife:

> There would be mornings where he would just tell me he can't get up and get out of bed and he said, "I can't go on living." There was one night where I could tell, I don't know if he was drunk or what, but he was just not all there and he sounded like a little kid and just telling me, "I'm scared, Marisa, I'm scared," and I would say, "What are you scared of; what's going on?" And he's like, "I don't know what to do; I'm scared of my thoughts."

Barret Robbins, who played for the Oakland Raiders, is a diagnosed bipolar sufferer. He has been linked to steroid use and has had various run-ins with the law. Police issued a warrant for his arrest in September 2007, but he has not been found. In interviews, Robbins's ex-wife has said she thinks his erratic behavior could be blamed on his bipolar disorder.

> And I asked him, "Are you having bad thoughts? Are you
> thinking about hurting yourself?" And he started crying
> and said, "Yes I am."[3]

Bipolar disorder cost Robbins his career in the NFL. In 2003 Robbins's team, the Oakland Raiders, prepared to play in the Super Bowl. A few days before the game, Robbins disappeared. He had gone on a drinking binge and tried to commit suicide. Suspended from the team, Robbins watched the game from his hospital room. He was eventually cut from the team.

Long History of Suffering

Manic depression has plagued mankind for thousands of years. The ancient Greek physician Hippocrates first diagnosed patients with bipolar symptoms in 400 B.C., calling the disorder "mania and melancholia." Practicing some 500 years later, another Greek physician, Aretaeus of Cappadocia, wrote this about his bipolar patients:

> Some patients with mania are cheerful—they laugh,
> play, dance day and night, and stroll through the market, sometimes with a garland on their head, as if they
> had won a game: these patients do not worry their relatives. But others fly into a rage. . . . The manifestations
> of mania are countless. Some manics, who are intelligent
> and well educated, deal with astronomy, although they
> never studied it, with philosophy [they are self-taught]
> and they consider poetry a gift of muses.[4]

In 1854 French physician Jules Falret defined the symptoms of the illness, labeling it *folie circulaire*, which means "circular insanity." Although psychiatric medicine was far less advanced in Falret's day than it is today, Falret correctly theorized that the condition could be inherited from one's parents. He also observed degrees of the disorder in his patients, noting that some were more manic or depressed than others. In 1896 a German psychiatrist, Emil Kraepelin, first used the term *manic depression* in a textbook on mental illnesses.

Over the years mental health experts further defined the symptoms of manic depression. In 1980, in a revision of its *Diagnostic and Statis-*

tical Manual of Mental Disorders, the American Psychiatric Association renamed the condition *bipolar disorder* (although *manic depression* is still commonly used).

What Causes Bipolar Disorders?

According to the National Institute of Mental Health, if a child has one parent who is bipolar, that child has as much as a 33 percent chance of developing the disorder. If both parents are manic depressive, the likelihood that the child will be bipolar rises to as high as 75 percent.

While those factors may seem to suggest that it is easy to diagnose bipolar disorder based on a patient's family history, that is not always the case. Many families keep mental illness hidden, afraid of the stigma that society places on such patients. Therefore, if a doctor examining a child asks the parent if there is a history of bipolar disorder in the family, he or she may not give the physician a true answer.

Since bipolar disorders tend to run in families, mental health experts believe there may be a genetic link among patients—that manic depression is hardwired into their DNA. Says psychiatrist and author Wes Burgess, "When scientists compare the DNA of individuals with bipolar disorder with the DNA from their family members who do not have the disease, they find that certain genes are associated with bipolar disorder."[5]

> " Bipolar disorder, also known as manic depression, is a mental illness characterized by dramatic mood swings that range from extreme euphoria to deep depression. "

In fact, genetic scientists suspect bipolar patients share common genes. Scientists are not sure how the genes cause a bipolar patient's irrational behavior, but they believe the bipolar genes may trigger chemical imbalances in the brain. For example, the adrenal glands of bipolar patients are known to secrete large quantities of the hormone cortisol, which regulates how the body reacts to stress.

Also, the brain cells, or neurons, of bipolar patients contain an overabundance of the chemical calcium. Calcium is an important component of the human body—it helps keep bones strong—but an overabundance of calcium in brain cells has been found to inhibit neurological functions.

Bipolar disorder may also have social or cultural causes. Somebody who grows up in a household where manic and depressive episodes are common may come to believe that such conduct is a normal way of living one's life.

Roots in Childhood

There are three main categories of bipolar disorder. In most cases, patients are diagnosed as bipolar I, bipolar II and hypomania, or cyclothymic disorder, based on the frequency and severity of their symptoms. In bipolar disorder I, patients experience intense degrees of mania and depression; the episodes are usually the most severe of the three major categories. In bipolar disorder II and hypomania, patients undergo long periods of depression followed by brief periods of hypomania. Hypomania is similar to mania, but the periods of euphoria are less severe than what a patient experiences during a bipolar I manic episode and do not last as long. Cyclothymic disorder is not as severe as the other forms of bipolar disorder; essentially, cyclothymic patients are never really too happy and never really too depressed, but they tend to be grumpy a lot of the time.

> " About 2.6 percent of the American population over the age of 18, or about 5.7 million people, are believed to suffer from bipolar disorders to some degree. "

Bipolar disorders can manifest themselves in childhood, where dramatic mood swings may occur several times a day. In children, bipolar disorders are often misdiagnosed as other childhood mental health issues. Frequently, bipolar children are believed to suffer from attention deficit hyperactive disorder, in which children are inattentive, impulsive, and hyperactive. Many parents and doctors also miss the symptoms of bipolar disorders because they think it is normal for young children to be moody, giddy, and full of energy. And in most cases, that truly is normal behavior for children.

Still, there is no question that many manic depressive patients do not receive definitive diagnoses of bipolar disorder until they are adults. Since the mid-1990s, though, mental health professionals have come to recognize the symptoms of bipolar disorder in children and have taken steps to control their symptoms. In 1995 a groundbreaking study at Massachusetts General Hospital first raised the notion that bipolar disorders were a lot more common in children than psychiatrists had previously believed. "Back then it was considered so rare in children that you might see one in your entire career," says child psychiatrist Janet Wozniak, a coauthor of the Massachusetts study. "But we'd been blind to children who were right in front of us."[6] Four years after the Massachusetts study, psychiatrist Demitri Papolos and his wife, Janice, coauthored the book *The Bipolar Child*, in which they suggested that at least a million bipolar children have been misdiagnosed with attention deficit hyperactive disorder.

> **In 1854 French physician Jules Falret defined the symptoms of the illness, labeling it *folie circulaire*, which means "circular insanity."**

Nevertheless, the issue of bipolar disorder in children remains very much in dispute among mental health professionals. Some physicians continue to harbor doubts about whether young children can truly be bipolar. Moreover, they are concerned about the methods of treating bipolar disorders in young children. As in adults, the primary treatment for bipolar disorders in children are daily doses of mood-stabilizing drugs, which they suggest could be a harsh regimen for young children. Says April Prewitt, a Massachusetts child psychologist who questions the diagnoses of bipolar disorders in young children, "It has become a diagnosis *du jour*. . . . Not only is the diagnosis being made incorrectly, but it's being made in younger and younger children."[7]

Mile-a-Minute Euphoria

Terri Cheney, a California attorney and author, provides a typical example of a bipolar patient who spent years suffering through her mood swings because doctors failed to recognize her manic depressive symptoms. "I first started getting depressed when I was sixteen," she says. "I couldn't get out of bed for three weeks. At 27, I was diagnosed with major depression and that was the wrong diagnosis."[8]

Cheney worked in Hollywood as an entertainment lawyer, representing celebrities in their negotiations with motion picture studios. The lifestyle was high-powered; meetings could go late into the night, followed by long bouts of drinking and hard partying.

Cheney believes her doctors misdiagnosed her with depression because they failed to recognize her manic periods, thinking that her mile-a-minute euphoric episodes were simply a part of her lifestyle. "I was 34 when I was diagnosed with manic depression," she says. "It takes people a long time to see the pattern that emerges in your life."[9]

How Do Bipolar Disorders Affect People?

Bipolar patients tend to engage in risky behavior, particularly substance abuse—as many as 80 percent of bipolar patients turn to alcohol or drugs. In the depressive phase, bipolar patients may drink or use drugs to help themselves feel better; in the manic phase, they may abuse substances in the belief that drugs and alcohol enhance their feelings of euphoria.

> "Bipolar disorders can manifest themselves in childhood, where dramatic mood swings may occur several times a day. In children, bipolar disorders are often misdiagnosed as other childhood mental health issues."

Representative Patrick J. Kennedy of Rhode Island first started exhibiting bipolar symptoms as a teenager. That is also when he first started abusing alcohol. Growing up in a political family—his father is Senator Edward M. Kennedy of Massachusetts—Patrick Kennedy entered politics himself at the age of 21 when he won election to the Rhode Island State Assembly; in 1994, at the age of 27, he won election to Congress.

As a member of Congress, he maintained a busy schedule, particularly in the 2000 elections when he campaigned hard to elect Democrats to House seats throughout the United States. But he was also drinking

Author Marya Hornbacher, seen here in her home office with her medication, has suffered from bipolar disorder for her entire life. An estimated 5.7 million Americans are bipolar, but the number could be much higher because psychiatrists often misdiagnose the illness as depression.

heavily and abusing prescription painkillers. In 2000—evidently under the influence of a substance while also in the throes of a manic episode—he argued loudly with an airport security officer who refused to let him pass an oversize bag through an X-ray scanner. In 2006, while under the influence of a prescription painkiller, he crashed his car two blocks from the U.S. Capitol in Washington. After the accident, he acknowledged that the crash as well as the incident at the airport was attributable to a combination of bipolar disorder, heavy drinking, and drug abuse.

Following the 2006 accident, Kennedy checked himself into a drug and alcohol treatment center. "I've got to do total abstinence, period," he says. "From now on, obviously, I'm a very public face with addiction and alcoholism written on my head."[10]

Another substance frequently abused by bipolar patients is tobacco—many manic depressives are heavy smokers. Mental health experts believe bipolar patients crave the rush often provided by nicotine.

High Suicide Risk

The suicide rate among bipolar patients is incredibly high—as many as 15 percent of manic depressives take their own lives. Compared with the rest of the population, that is an astronomical rate. According to the U.S. Centers for Disease Control and Prevention, the overall suicide rate in the United States is 11 per 100,000 people. It means that in a city with a population of 100,000, 11 people will take their own lives. But in a city of 100,000 bipolar patients, 15,000 will commit suicide.

Mental health experts tie in the high suicide rate among bipolar patients with their high substance abuse rate—studies have shown that more than 60 percent of the manic depressives who take their own lives were abusing alcohol and drugs at the time of their deaths. "Patients with bipolar disorder and alcoholism are in a very precarious situation," says University of Pittsburgh psychiatry professor Ihsan Salloum. "They have high disability rates and ultimately the presence of these two disorders lead to high death rates."[11]

Odd and Unusual Behaviors

Suicide and substance abuse are among the riskiest types of behavior in which bipolar patients may engage, but during their manic phases they may engage in all manner of other odd and unusual behaviors. Those behaviors could include spending sprees, promiscuity, and dressing in inappropriate clothing. Bipolar patients may become angry and violent for no apparent reason. They may suffer from paranoia, meaning they do not trust others and feel people mean them harm.

Bipolar patients have difficulty maintaining relationships. Their performance in school or work is usually poor.

> Bipolar patients tend to engage in risky behavior, particularly substance abuse—as many as 80 percent of bipolar patients turn to alcohol or drugs.

These behaviors often occur during the manic phases. During their depressive episodes, bipolar patients usually feel sorrow for the way they acted. Their self-esteem is low.

What Treatments Are Available for Bipolar Disorders?

Bipolar disorders require lifelong treatment, mostly through drug therapy and lifestyle changes. The most commonly prescribed drug for bipolar disorder is lithium, which has been administered for treatment of bipolar symptoms for about 40 years.

Lithium—actually, chemical salts extracted from the metal lithium—can be employed as a mood-stabilizing drug. It affects the flow of neurotransmitters, the chemicals that carry messages from brain cell to brain cell. Specifically, lithium balances the flow of the neurotransmitter glutamate in the brain. Glutamate is instrumental in the brain's ability to form memories.

> " The suicide rate among bipolar patients is incredibly high—as many as 15 percent of manic depressives take their own lives. "

Bipolar patients are also urged to make lifestyle changes—to give up drugs, alcohol, and tobacco, and perhaps find different places to live or different jobs in which the stresses in their lives would be reduced. Many bipolar patients also undergo psychotherapy to help them identify the social situations that spark their episodes. Meeting with psychiatrists individually or in group sessions, they learn to recognize the symptoms of bipolar disorders and how to manage them without flying into manic episodes or falling into deep states of depression.

New Outlook

Film star Linda Hamilton, who portrayed Sarah Connor in the *Terminator* films, has learned to control her bipolar episodes through drug therapy, psychotherapy, and lifestyle changes such as exercise and giving up alcohol. Hamilton suffered through mood swings for years. At the age of 22, she was diagnosed with depression, but the doctor did not recognize the manic side of her illness. As she was finding success as an actress, she was also suffering through 2 turbulent marriages in which she abused alcohol. Finally, at the age of 40, she saw another doctor, who diagnosed her as having a bipolar disorder.

Hamilton gave up alcohol, took up gardening and table tennis, committed herself to a regular exercise routine, takes her medication faithfully and keeps her appointments with her psychotherapist. Now in her fifties, Hamilton believes her bipolar symptoms are under control. "I feel solid," she says, "but it took me twenty years of struggling and suffering and hard work to get here."[12]

What Does the Future Hold for Bipolar Patients?

Hamilton proves that bipolar patients do not have to face lifetimes of dramatic and unexpected mood swings. Moreover, scientists are hoping to find a genetic fingerprint that may help people learn they are bipolar before their symptoms become apparent. Armed with such knowledge, bipolar patients may be able to learn to recognize and control their symptoms, saving themselves years of anguish.

In the treatment of bipolar patients, there is a new emphasis on family education. In prior years, bipolar patients often found themselves confronting their illnesses alone, but now mental health experts urge family members to take an active role in the treatments of their loved ones, helping them recognize the symptoms and confronting their manic and depressive episodes with positive reinforcement. Says University of Colorado psychology professor David J. Miklowitz, "If you combine medication and family focused therapy, you get quicker recoveries and longer intervals of wellness. The relapses are less common, and [patients'] functioning improves."[13]

There is a lot of hope for manic depressives. Medications are effective, and other treatment techniques, such as family-focused therapy, have helped many bipolar patients control their symptoms. Still, there are many bipolar patients who continue to suffer through the wild mood swings of manic depression. They endure the symptoms as undiagnosed bipolar patients, wondering why they continually ride a roller coaster of periods of euphoria and depression. These patients and others face a lifetime of uncertainty, broken relationships with loved ones, substance abuse, and, in many cases, early deaths through suicide.

What Are Bipolar Disorders and What Are the Symptoms?

"At my lowest, I would feel it coming on, like hot tar welling up from my bowels into my throat, bubbling and churning. First, the agitation, then the anger, the grief and the voices, creepy and hissing, so loud that it was as if someone was yelling beside me."

—Autumn Stringam, bipolar patient and author of the memoir *A Promise of Hope*.

Mood Disorders

Bipolar disorders are regarded as mood disorders. Everybody has moods—people may be happy, sad, pensive, optimistic, pessimistic, fearful, and calm. It is not unusual for people's moods to change many times during the course of a day. In most cases, mood changes are prompted by external events. If somebody is feeling low and they receive some good news, chances are their mood will brighten.

A person is afflicted with a mood disorder if his or her mood changes because of mental illness. In addition to bipolar disorders, depression is also regarded as a mood disorder. Of course, depression is also a component of bipolar disorder. About 12 million American adults suffer from depression alone; another 5.7 million suffer from episodes of mania and depression.

Another term for mood disorder is *affective disorder*, which stems from the Latin word *affectus*, which means a mental quality opposite to reason. In addition to depression and bipolar disorders, there are other ailments that are classified as affective disorders, some of which include physical symptoms. Migraine headaches, for example, may be prompted by a change in mood. Irritable bowel syndrome, in which the patient may experience abdominal pains, may be attributed to changes in mood. Fibromyalgia, which causes muscle soreness and joint pain in patients, may flare up because of changes in mood. In these cases, anger or another emotion may cause patients to develop headaches, stomachaches, or muscle pain.

Depression and Mania

In bipolar disorders, patients experience wide swings in their moods. To be bipolar is to bounce between the two extreme opposite poles of mood: depression and mania.

Depressed people are afflicted with feelings of sadness, hopelessness, and inadequacy. They may feel so low that they cannot summon the strength to rise from bed in the morning. They lack the ability to enjoy life. Many depressed people have no appetites and are unable to sleep soundly. They may feel worthless and harbor feelings of extreme guilt. They may have trouble concentrating on problems and making up their minds. They think a lot

> A person is afflicted with a mood disorder if his or her mood changes because of mental illness.

about their own deaths and often contemplate suicide. In describing her episodes of depression, author and bipolar patient Marya Hornbacher recalled her desire simply to stay hidden in bed:

> The world outside swells and presses at the walls, trying to reach me, trying to eat me alive. I must stay here in the pocket of my sheets. . . . I will not face the world, with its lights and noise, its confusion, the way I lose myself in its crowds. The way I disappear. I am the invisible girl. I am make-believe. I am not really there.[14]

In contrast, most patients going through episodes of mania are cheer-ful—perhaps at inappropriate times—and they may find themselves talk-ing nonstop. Others experience irritability and shortness of temper. They may strike up long and intimate con-versations with complete strangers. During their manic phases, they have little need for sleep. They have expanded egos—extreme confidence in themselves to perform tasks they may be incapable of carrying out. (If they fail, their inability to meet their own expectations may trigger long phases of depression, guilt, and low self-esteem.) Bipolar patient Barbara Arner of New Jersey recalled her first manic episode, which occurred when she was a 19-year-old college student:

> **To be bipolar is to bounce between the two extreme opposite poles of mood: depression and mania.**

> I stopped eating; I was running all over the place, spend-ing money for no reason. I started acting out in class. The school sent counselors to my dorm room, which made me scared and angry. It happened so suddenly; they sent over an ambulance and broke into my room. There were police officers, trying to get me downstairs. They cor-nered me, handcuffed me, and suddenly I screamed out, "I know what my problem is! I have bipolar disorder!"[15]

Bipolar Disorder I

In 1994 the American Psychiatric Association determined that there are three main categories of bipolar disorder. The most common form, bipo-lar I, is characterized by full-blown manic episodes followed by deep fits of depression. Usually, periods of mania last a week or even months, while episodes of depression can typically last six months to a year.

In conversation, bipolar patients may talk quickly and jump from one topic to another. "At the time, I didn't consider my behavior strange," says Sol Wachtler, a former New York state judge whose career was ruined by bipolar disorder. "I thought [others] were bizarre, not me. 'I'm not talk-ing too fast,' I'd say. 'You're listening too slow.'"[16]

In the depressive phase, patients live in a dark, troubled world. Before he died in 2002, Academy Award–winning actor Rod Steiger, a bipolar patient, described his depressive episodes:

> You have moments when you're locked in an ever-increasing terror. You begin to doubt your sanity. When you're depressed, there's no calendar. There are no dates, there's no day, there's no night, there's no seconds, there's no minutes, there's nothing. You're just existing in this cold, murky, ever-heavy atmosphere, like they put you inside this vial of mercury.[17]

Bipolar II and Hypomania

In the category of bipolar disorder known as bipolar II and hypomania, the symptoms are regarded as less intense than those of bipolar I. Nevertheless, bipolar II patients suffer through long periods of depression interrupted by episodes of hypomania.

Because hypomania is not as severe as mania, doctors often misdiagnose bipolar II patients as suffering from depression only. In such a case of misdiagnosis, the doctor would typically prescribe an antidepressant drug such as Prozac, which could have a devastating affect on bipolar patients, enhancing their symptoms rather than controlling them.

Moreover, even if the doctor or family members recognize mood swings from depression to hypomania, the patient may deny there is something wrong because he or she feels very good during an episode of hypomania. According to Nassir Ghaemi, associate professor of psychiatry at Emory University in Atlanta, Georgia, during the hypomania phase it is possible for a bipolar II patient to function on a level

> " The most common form, bipolar I, is characterized by full-blown manic episodes followed by deep fits of depression. "

that friends and coworkers may find acceptable—the patient's speech may not be quite as fast and the patient's attention may be a bit more focused than one would find in a bipolar I patient. "With bipolar II, the sufferer won't become so grandiose that he or she loses a job," says Ghaemi. "They will be much more active than normal, but they won't have problems due to those activities."[18]

Certainly, though, bipolar II patients must still endure devastating episodes of depression. As for their hypomania periods, mental health experts warn that unless the patients receive treatment, the hypomania episodes can progress into much more severe manic episodes.

> **Because hypomania is not as severe as mania, doctors often misdiagnose bipolar II patients as suffering from depression only.**

Some physicians believe that seasonal affective disorder is also a form of bipolar II. In seasonal affective disorder, patients feel depressed during the winter months—possibly due to chemical imbalances in their brains that are triggered by a lack of sunlight—but in the springtime they recover and experience episodes of hypomania.

Living with Hypomania

TV journalist Jane Pauley has been diagnosed as a bipolar patient who suffers from episodes of hypomania. The former host of the *Today* show and wife of *Doonesbury* cartoonist Garry Trudeau, Pauley was first diagnosed with depression in 2001. She was treated with antidepressant drugs, which she believed were working because her bouts of depression were often followed by feelings of euphoria and periods of creativity. "Feelings came shooting in and out at the speed of bullet trains," she says, "along with ideas, followed by phone calls that produced action plans. Mostly it was good, but I was aware that I was in hyper mode from the moment I woke up at 6:30 and started the day with a bang."[19]

In reality, the antidepressant drugs weren't managing her depression—her feelings of anxiety and inadequacy were instead followed by episodes of hypomania. After a few months, she returned to her psychiatrist and told him she had been thinking a lot about death. Believing that she was suicidal, Pauley's doctor urged her to check herself in to a residential mental health institution. At first she resisted but later agreed and spent three weeks in a New York City facility.

"The rush of ideas that had impressed many people and worried Garry was symptomatic of hypomania. This was a new word for me, which I interpreted—incorrectly—to mean 'big time mania,'" Pauley says. "When I looked up hypomania (hypo meaning 'mild,' not 'big-time'), I recognized myself right away."[20]

Eventually, Pauley was correctly diagnosed with a bipolar disorder and put on the proper medication. Since her release from the institution, she has been able to function normally. She has written her memoirs, *Skywriting: A Life Out of the Blue*, and hosted a TV talk show, *The Jane Pauley Show*, which aired until 2005.

Cyclothymic Disorder

The third major category of bipolar disorder, cyclothymic disorder, is less severe than bipolar I and bipolar II. Indeed, the manic periods among these patients are characterized more by irritability than by euphoria. Still, periods of cyclothymic disorder last at least two years, with single episodes occurring for a few days or weeks or more.

One cyclothymic patient, writer Andrew Solomon, said it did not take much to tip him between periods of lucidity and irritability. He recalled receiving a phone call that made him annoyed. At the conclusion of the call, he slammed the phone down so hard that it broke in two. A short time later, he insulted a friend—then felt guilty for a week, phoning her and constantly apologizing. "When something happens, I might have an exaggerated response to it,"[21] says Solomon.

Cyclothymic disorder may progress into bipolar I or bipolar II. In fact, half of all cyclothymics go on to develop the more severe forms of the illness, mostly because they go undiagnosed as cyclothymics until they have already moved on to the bipolar I or II stages of the illness. Solomon first started noticing his mood swings as a teenager, but he was not diagnosed as a cyclothymic until the age of 39. Now, with medication and psychotherapy, Solomon has

> " Believing that she was suicidal, Jane Pauley's doctor urged her to check herself in to a residential mental health institution. "

learned to control his mood swings and is not likely to progress into the next stage of the disorder. "My moods have become more logical and rational and less extreme," he says. "They're easier for me and other people to live with."[22]

Rapid Cycling and Mixed Mania

In all bipolar patients, the severity and lengths of their manic and depressive episodes vary widely. Indeed, within the diagnoses of the three major categories of bipolar disorder, symptoms differ from patient to patient. For example, bipolar I and II patients who experience four or more episodes of depression and mania a year suffer from what is known as rapid cycling—as many as 15 percent of bipolar patients will experience rapid cycling during the course of their illnesses. Sometimes the cycling of mood swings will be so rapid that the patient will bounce from severe depression to extreme euphoria or irritability in the course of a few hours. Marya Hornbacher says it is not unusual for her moods to swing from depressive in the morning to manic at night:

> " Sometimes the cycling of mood swings will be so rapid that the patient will bounce from severe depression to extreme euphoria or irritability in the course of a few hours. "

> I turn into a monster, screaming at my mother, getting more and more agitated every evening, ramping up into rabid, nasty mania by night. I go crashing out the door, headed for God knows where. In the morning, she finds me lying in bed with my face to the wall. She opens the blinds. *You have to have light*, she says. *No. Please close them. Please.* Depression settles in for the day. By evening, I am nuts again, and go out into the night, and come back again to lie in bed, hiding from the sun.[23]

Many bipolar patients also suffer from what are known as mixed mania episodes, in which symptoms of both depression and mania are present. A patient suffering from mixed mania will be excited, agitated, and depressed—but not euphoric. Instead, in a mixed mania episode the feeling of euphoria is replaced by irritability. It is believed that as many as 45 percent of bipolar I and II patients will experience episodes of mixed mania during their lifetimes.

Among the patients who suffer from the most severe cases of bipolar disorder are those said to be "mood-incongruent." They laugh when hearing that a friend or loved one has died, or they fall into a depressive episode when given good news.

Sometimes, a patient's symptoms of bipolar disorder do not seem to fit neatly into any of the three major categories. In those cases, doctors designate the patient as suffering from "bipolar disorder not otherwise specified." Patients who are so designated may experience mood swings that do not seem to last as long as what is typically found in bipolar I or II. Or the patient may experience episodes of hypomania without automatically lapsing into depression.

Clearly, no two bipolar cases are alike. The fact that many doctors continue to misdiagnose bipolar disorder as depression proves the illness is still surrounded by many mysteries. That is particularly true for the patients, who are often shocked when their doctors tell them they suffer from a bipolar disorder even though, at the moment, they may be feeling very good about themselves.

Primary Source Quotes*

What Are Bipolar Disorders and What Are the Symptoms?

66 They are prone to change their minds readily; to become base, mean-spirited, illiberal, and in a little time, perhaps, simple, extravagant, munificent, not from any virtue of the soul, but from the changeableness of the disease. But if the illness becomes more urgent . . . they complain of life and desire to die. 99

— Aretaeus of Cappadocia, quoted in Jerome Goopman, "What's Normal?" *New Yorker*, April 9, 2007.

Greek physician Aretaeus studied bipolar disorder in the first century A.D.

66 Bipolar disorder causes much more than simply mania and depression. It can also cause feelings of irritability, anger, jealousy, resentment, anxiety, avoidance, embarrassment, fear, inadequacy, regret, and confusion. 99

—Wes Burgess, *The Bipolar Handbook*. New York: Avery, 2006.

Burgess is an author and psychiatrist practicing in Los Angeles, California.

* Editor's Note: While the definition of a primary source can be narrowly or broadly defined, for the purposes of Compact Research, a primary source consists of: 1) results of original research presented by an organization or researcher; 2) eyewitness accounts of events, personal experience, or work experience; 3) first-person editorials offering pundits' opinions; 4) government officials presenting political plans and/or policies; 5) representatives of organizations presenting testimony or policy.

Primary Source Quotes

❝Manic depression distorts moods and thoughts, incites dreadful behaviors, destroys the basis of rational thought, and too often erodes the desire and will to live.❞

—Kay Redfield Jamison, quoted in National Institute of Mental Health, *Bipolar Disorder*, January 2007. www.nimh.nih.gov.

Jamison is a professor of psychology at Johns Hopkins University in Baltimore, Maryland.

....

❝There was a time when I wasn't allowed to be alone with my three-year-old son. I suffered from a severe form of the disorder characterized by extreme highs and lows in mood. I'd go through periods of irrational, grandiose thoughts and then depression.❞

—Autumn Stringam, "My New Ordinary Life," *Chatelaine*, May 2008.

A Canadian mother of four, Stringam wrote a memoir of bipolar disorder titled *A Promise of Hope*.

....

❝You get beautifully and painfully thin on the road up to mania. Eating simply doesn't occur to you because there are too many other thoughts occupying your mind, important thoughts, thoughts that could change the world if only you could stop long enough to jot them down.❞

—Terri Cheney, *Manic: A Memoir*. New York: William Morrow, 2008.

Cheney is a bipolar patient, California attorney, and the author of *Manic: A Memoir*.

....

❝When I was manic, I was drinking, spending excessively, out of control. I entered into nightmare relationships. I was looking for the next extreme thing to do. One day, I left my job and felt that I had a new purpose in life: to drive as fast as I possibly could somewhere.❞

—Marya Hornbacher, quoted in Michelle Tan and Michelle Taubr, "Britney in Crisis," *People*, September 21, 2008.

Hornbacher, a bipolar patient, is the author of the memoir *Madness: A Bipolar Life*.

❝Bipolar disorder is challenging to diagnose because individuals can cover up the symptoms of the illness or may recognize only their depression, not the manic phase of the disorder. It is also important to be able to distinguish bipolar disorder from major depression because a mistaken diagnosis can result in the wrong therapy and unstable moods for years.❞

—John D. Port, quoted in Patrick Perry, "New Strategy for Diagnosing Bipolar Disorder," *Saturday Evening Post*, March/April 2005.

Port is an assistant professor of radiology at the Mayo Clinic in Rochester, Minnesota.

❝When you're hypomanic and you feel euphoric and on top of the world, who wants to take a medication that will take that away?❞

—Prentiss Price, quoted in Stacey Colino, "Cyclothymia: Restoring the Balance," *Saturday Evening Post*, November/December 2006.

Price is a psychologist at Georgia Southern University in Statesboro, Georgia, and the author of *The Cyclothymia Workbook*.

66 **Doctors have specific criteria regarding mania and hypomania. I was never at the level of mania, though I don't know how close I was.** 99

—Jane Pauley, quoted in Patrick Perry, "Jane Pauley: Tackling the Stigma of Bipolar Disorder," *Saturday Evening Post*, March/April 2007.

Pauley, a TV journalist, is a bipolar patient and the author of *Skywriting: A Life Out of the Blue*.

66 **Sometimes, when talking to people, I'll tell them I've just had a lot of coffee, even though it's not true, because I know I fire off in all directions, and I can talk to you about anything ... and one thing I say to people is that, of course, I live near the edge.** 99

—Laurence McKinney, quoted in Benedict Carey, "Hypomanic? Absolutely. But Oh So Productive!" *New York Times*, March 22, 2005.

McKinney, a business consultant from Boston, suffers from hypomania.

66 **My moods can switch within minutes. On the outside, I have fast, loud speech, and am an energetic personality. I can cry at the drop of a hat, speaking hard truths with little or no filter, yelling, and pacing. On the inside, I have racing thoughts, fear or panic.** 99

—Kelly Barratt, quoted in Michelle Roberts, "The Many Faces and Facets of BP," *BP*, Summer 2007. www.bphope.com.

Bipolar patient Barratt is a corporate financial analyst who lives in Austin, Texas.

66 **I have been angry, enraged, depressed, elated, and even suicidal. I have offended and lost many friends. Rapid cycling is hard and my mood changes come without warning.** 99

—Glenn Denton, quoted in Michelle Roberts, "The Many Faces and Facets of BP," *BP*, Summer 2007. www.bphope.com.

Denton, a bipolar patient, is a respiratory therapist who lives in Avenel, New Jersey.

Facts and Illustrations

What Are Bipolar Disorders and What Are the Symptoms?

- Many people first experience bipolar symptoms by the **age of 25**, although it is not unusual for the symptoms to emerge in childhood or when the patients reach their 40s or 50s.

- Although men and women suffer from bipolar disorders in roughly equal numbers, **three times** as many women as men are rapid cyclers.

- **Twenty percent** of teens diagnosed with major depression are likely to develop bipolar disorders within five years of the onset of their depressive symptoms.

- A study of manic depression patients by seven American universities found that **15 percent** of the men and **29 percent** of the women suffered from bipolar II and hypomania.

- An estimated **7 percent** of Americans—about 21 million people—suffer from affective disorders.

- Worldwide, more than **250 million** people may suffer from bipolar disorders.

- Most bipolar patients will not be correctly diagnosed for at least **10 years** following the onset of their symptoms.

Most Bipolar Episodes First Hit Patients in Their Early Twenties

A joint study by the University of Chicago, Johns Hopkins University, the National Institute of Mental Health, and the University of Heidelberg in Germany studied 295 bipolar patients. They concluded that most patients experience their first symptoms in their early twenties, and that symptoms can last 20 years or more. During the course of their illnesses, bipolar II patients may experience nearly 50 episodes of hypomania (a mania of less intensity) as well as 17 episodes of depression.

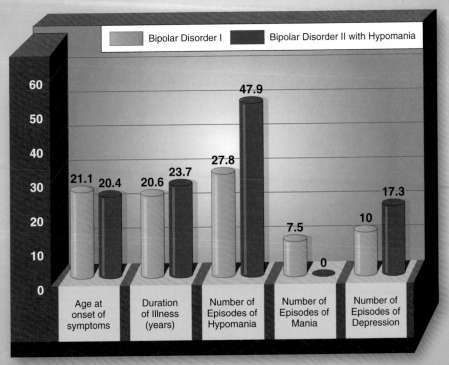

Source: Maria E. Fisfalen et al., "Familial Variation in Episode Frequency in Bipolar Affective Disorder," *American Journal of Psychiatry*, July 2005.

- Most bipolar patients will visit **three separate psychiatrists** before finding a doctor who recognizes the symptoms of manic depression.

- About **25 percent** of bipolar patients will go on spending sprees or engage in impulsive sexual relationships during their manic phases.

- Of the **5.7 million** Americans who suffer from bipolar disorder, about **2.2 million** are cyclothymia patients.

Rapid Cycling Often Arrives in the Teen Years

Rapid cyclers, people who have 4 or more episodes within 12 months, compose about 20 percent of bipolar patients, according to a study by the University of Colorado. However, rapid cyclers experience their symptoms earlier than other bipolar patients, and they have more depressive, manic, and hypomanic episodes per year than bipolar patients who are not rapid cyclers.

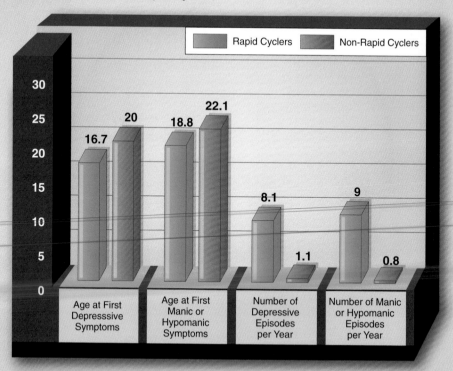

Source: Christopher D. Schneck et al., "Phenomenology of Rapid-Cycling Bipolar Disorder: Data from the First 500 Participants in the Systematic Treatment Enhancement Program," *American Journal of Psychiatry*, October 2004.

Sadness and Reduced Sleep Among the Most Severe Bipolar Symptoms

Researchers for Massachusetts General Hospital and Harvard Medical School rated the severity of symptoms for 477 bipolar patients on a scale of 0 to 4. Sadness and tension were among the most severe symptoms. Bipolar patients also have trouble concentrating and sleeping, and many think a lot about suicide.

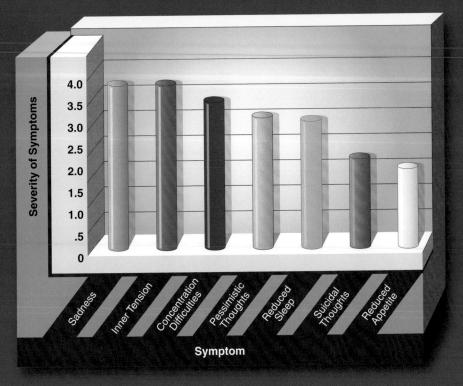

Source: Roy H. Perlis et al., "Clinical Features of Bipolar Depression Versus Major Depressive Disorder in Large Multicenter Trials," *American Journal of Psychiatry*, February 2006.

- A third of the **3.4 million children** and teens in America who have been diagnosed with depression may actually be suffering from bipolar disorders.

- Presidents **John Adams, Theodore Roosevelt, and Lyndon B. Johnson** suffered from bipolar disorders. Abraham Lincoln's wife, Mary Todd Lincoln, is also believed to have been bipolar.

The Most Severe Bipolar Cases

Patients who suffer from the most severe cases of bipolar disorders are said to be "mood-incongruent"—they laugh at the news that a friend or loved one has died, or they lapse into depression when given a raise and promotion at work. A study by 11 universities and the National Institute of Mental Health looked at some of the characteristics of mood-incongruent bipolar patients, and found that they experience an onset of symptoms earlier than other bipolar patients, and that they have more depressive and manic episodes. Also, they tend to abuse drugs in larger numbers and are at a higher risk than other patients to commit suicide.

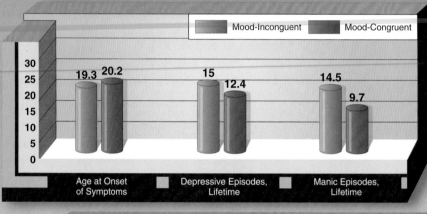

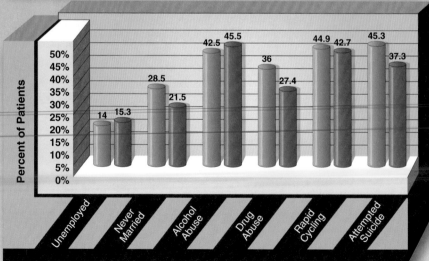

Source: Fernando S. Goes et al., "Mood-Incongruent Psychotic Features in Bipolar Disorder," *American Journal of Psychology*, February 2007.

What Causes Bipolar Disorders?

> **While most girls my age get moody from hormones, my mood swings came from a brain difference that caused 'mood seizures.' These mood swings were more dramatic than what's normal for pre-teens. It's kind of like the difference between having a cold and having pneumonia.**

—Ivy, a 13-year-old Massachusetts girl who has been diagnosed with a bipolar disorder.

Chemical Imbalances

Although there are many factors that contribute to bipolar disorders, all bipolar patients suffer from chemical imbalances in their brains and bodies. These imbalances can be found in various hormones as well as neurotransmitters that flow through the brains and bodies of patients, regulating how they react to stress and other emotional situations.

Hormones are chemicals that enable the body's organs to carry out their functions. One group of hormones is secreted in the thyroid gland, which is located at the base of the neck. These hormones, such as thyroxine, help provide the body with energy. If the thyroid gland produces too many hormones, the condition known as hyperthyroidism occurs. In hyperthyroidism, the body has too much energy to burn. Therefore, hyperthyroidism is suspected as a cause of the manic episodes in bipolar patients. On the other hand, if the thyroid gland produces too few hormones, the condition is known as hypothyroidism. In bipolar patients, hypothyroidism is believed to be a cause of depression. Says Peter Whybrow, professor of psychiatry at the University of California at Los Angeles, "Thyroid hormones have a powerful effect on brain physiology."[24]

Another group of hormones is secreted by the adrenal glands, which are found near the kidneys. Adrenal hormones, including adrenaline and cortisol, help the body react to stress. Oversecretions of cortisol and adrenaline have been found to trigger episodes of mania while too little of these hormones can result in depression.

Doctors suspect that the neurotransmitters produced by the brain may be out of balance in bipolar patients. Among the neurotransmitters affected by bipolar disorders are glutamate, which is instrumental in the brain's ability to form memories; serotonin, which controls sleep, mood, and appetite; dopamine, which regulates the release of hormones; and norepinephrine, which regulates responses to stress, anxiety, and memory. "Stress hormones are . . . only part of the picture," say Colorado psychologists David J. Milkowitz and Elizabeth L. George in their book *The Bipolar Teen*. "We know that among bipolar adults too much or too little of certain neurotransmitters is produced at different phases of the illness—which is why you may have heard bipolar disorder called a 'biochemical imbalance.'"[25]

> Although there are many factors that contribute to bipolar disorders, all bipolar patients suffer from chemical imbalances in their brains and bodies.

Other chemicals in the body are also suspected of causing bipolar episodes. For example, an overabundance of calcium in the brain cells is suspected of being at the root of bipolar disorders. Calcium is an important component of the body—it helps keep teeth and bones strong. Calcium can also be found in brain cells, where it helps maintain the electrical activity that transmits messages from neuron to neuron. When there is too much calcium in the brain cells, the neurons may become agitated. In bipolar patients, an overabundance of calcium is suspected as a trigger for manic episodes.

Hormonal Changes in Women

The stresses of pregnancy and childbirth, including hormonal changes, lack of sleep, and the pain of labor and delivery, may all have an impact on bipolar women. As far back as the nineteenth century, Emil Kraepelin noted an increased number of manic episodes in bipolar women shortly after they gave birth. Bipolar women are also known to lapse into depressive episodes following the births of their children. (The mood disorder known as postpartum depression is also common among women who are not bipolar.)

The female hormones estrogen and progesterone may have a lot to do with these mood swings. Estrogen promotes development of female sexual characteristics, while progesterone helps prepare the body for conception and pregnancy. Also, both hormones help regulate the menstrual cycle. It is common for many women to undergo imbalances in these hormones just before and during their menstrual cycles as well as during pregnancy and labor. Doctors believe that imbalances in estrogen and progesterone during these "hormonal transition periods" may hit bipolar women especially hard. Indeed, these hormonal balances may enhance episodes of rapid cycling in bipolar women. "Women need to be critically aware of changes in their moods during key life cycle events,"[26] says Sherry Marts, vice president of the Washington-based Society for Women's Health Research.

Moreover, a bipolar woman who wants to have children faces a significant dilemma: Obstetricians advise all women not to take drugs during their pregnancies for fear that the drugs may affect the development of their fetuses. In fact, the most common drug prescribed for bipolar disorders, lithium, can cause heart valve defects in fetuses. Sometimes a defect in a heart valve—which controls the amount of blood entering the heart—can be fatal to the infant. Martha Netoff, a bipolar woman from St. Louis Park, Minnesota, took lithium during her pregnancy and lost her baby due to a severe heart valve defect in the infant. "We were devastated,"[27] she says.

> " Adrenal hormones, including adrenaline and cortisol, help the body react to stress. Oversecretions of cortisol and adrenaline have been found to trigger episodes of mania. "

Doctors recommend that bipolar women take no lithium during the first trimester and only the lowest possible doses for the remainder of their pregnancies. Still, if a bipolar woman alters her mood stabilizing medication for several months, it is likely she will lapse into the mood swings of manic depression, which may be further inflamed by the stresses of pregnancy and childbirth. Says Netoff, "We want to try to have another child, but I am frightened that my drugs will hurt my next child. I, too, am afraid of having a major episode while pregnant if I go off my drugs. I've been suicidal before and never want to go back there again."[28]

Family History

Family history is a significant factor in determining whether a person will develop bipolar symptoms—according to the National Institute of Mental Health, as many as 33 percent of bipolar patients have at least one bipolar parent. That fact has prompted scientists to search for common genes among bipolar patients. Genes, which are composed of DNA molecules, are the basic components of people that make up who they are—whether they have blue eyes and brown hair, and whether they develop mental illnesses such as bipolar disorders. Genes are hereditary, meaning they are passed down from generation to generation.

The Pulitzer Prize–winning poet Anne Sexton spent years enduring symptoms of manic depression. She made several attempts at suicide, finally taking her own life in 1974 at the age of 45. At the time of Sexton's death, her daughter, Linda, was 21 years old.

> As far back as the nineteenth century, Emil Kraepelin noted an increased number of manic episodes in bipolar women shortly after they gave birth.

Nine years later, Linda Sexton was diagnosed with cyclothymic disorder. She found herself experiencing episodes of depression while trying to relate to her young children. To get over her feelings of depression, she would go on spending sprees—sometimes buying 10 pairs of shoes at a time. Later, she realized the spending sprees were episodes of hypomania. "I was having periods of depression during which I was unable to complete tasks and didn't feel like I had anything to offer my children, which was killing me because I considered them the most precious things in my life,"[29] she said.

As with her mother, Linda Sexton's symptoms continued to worsen. In 1996 doctors told her that her cyclothymic disorder had progressed to bipolar I.

While genetic factors may have a lot to do with whether people develop bipolar disorders, children are also influenced by life at home. Studies indicate that raising children in dysfunctional homes can help spark bipolar disorders. Children raised in an environment of bickering, depression, and risky behavior can develop similar symptoms. According to a 2006 study reported in the *American Journal of Psychiatry*, "Relationship risk factors—verbal abuse, witnessing of violence, physical or sexual maltreatment—play a role in the development of conduct disorder symptoms in younger children, dissociative and mood symptoms in young adults, and overt mood and anxiety disorders, as well as possible risk of physical disorders, by mid-adulthood."[30]

> **While genetic factors may have a lot to do with whether people develop bipolar disorders, children are also influenced by life at home. Studies indicate that raising children in dysfunctional homes can help spark bipolar disorders.**

Upsetting the Biological Clock

Bipolar patients are believed to have superfast biological clocks, the parts of the brain that tell them when it is morning and evening. The biological clock is located in the suprachiasmatic nucleus, or SCN, which is found in the hypothalamus. The hypothalamus is located deep in the center of the brain. One of its functions is to control sleep patterns.

The SCN controls the body's circadian rhythms, which let the body know when it is nighttime and daytime and, therefore, when it is time to go to bed and time to wake up. The circadian rhythms are constantly adjusting themselves as the days and nights grow longer or shorter according to the seasons. In bipolar patients, the SCN often malfunctions, throwing off the patient's circadian rhythms. That may help explain why bipolar patients, while in their manic phases, often need very little sleep.

On the other hand, bipolar patients who are in their depressive phases may stay in bed for days. "People might sleep all the time or not sleep at all," says University of Texas neuroscientist Colleen McClung. "Everyone on this planet has a 24-hour internal clock, and it is deeply ingrained in our biology."[31]

The hypothalamus is also part of a system in the body known as the hypothalamus-pituitary axis, which works with the adrenal glands to produce adrenaline. If the hypothalamus malfunctions and too much adrenaline is produced, the patient can experience an episode of mania; if too little adrenaline is produced, a period of depression could ensue.

Other Physiological Factors

Studies show that in bipolar patients, the frontal and temporal lobes of the brain as well as the portion of the brain known as the hippocampus lose neurons—in other words, these portions of the brain are shrinking. The frontal lobe helps the brain make decisions and controls emotions; among the functions of the temporal lobe are the control of speech and memory. The hippocampus also stores memories. Making poor decisions, emotional outbursts, forgetfulness, talking too fast—all can be symptoms of the manic phase of bipolar disorder. Even bipolar children, whose brains are still developing, show loss of brain cells in these components.

> **If the hypothalamus malfunctions and too much adrenaline is produced, the patient can experience an episode of mania; if too little adrenaline is produced, a period of depression could ensue.**

Scientists are not sure why the brains of bipolar patients lose neurons. They suggest that the stress on the brain caused by bipolar episodes may be responsible for killing neurons. Another theory suggests that the erosion of brain cells in bipolar patients may be genetic—that one of the inherited properties of the disease is the loss of neurons in the patient. Asks British psychiatrist Philip Timms, "Are the brain changes causing the disorder or is the disorder—and its associated stress—causing the brain changes?"[32]

Another component of the brain that may malfunction in bipolar patients is the amygdalae, the two almond-shaped balls of tissue near the ears. The amygdalae control judgment, responding during a person's "fight or flight" reaction, which usually occurs in a stressful situation. When under stress, the amygdalae help a person decide whether to stay and fight or to run away. In bipolar people the amygdalae respond abnormally, perhaps throwing a patient into a deep fit of depression over what may actually be a very mild threat. Amygdalae that are misfiring may have a lot to do with why a bipolar patient may display poor judgment and launch into impulsive acts such as spending sprees and casual sexual relationships.

Clearly, there is no single cause for bipolar disorders. In fact, a variety of factors may be at work: genetics, environment, chemical imbalances in the body and brain, and malfunctioning components of the brain all seem to play roles in the development of bipolar disorders. None of these factors are easy to measure, which helps explain why bipolar disorders are so hard to diagnose, particularly in children.

When someone who is feeling moody or depressed sees a psychiatrist, the doctor will ask the patient whether he or she has a family history of bipolar disorder. The doctor will then want to know what type of symptoms the patient is manifesting. Based on those symptoms and knowledge of family history, the psychiatrist will then make the diagnosis. It would be much easier for doctors to diagnose bipolar disorder if they were able to do so through a blood sample or other physiological method that could provide definitive evidence. At this point, no such reliable tests exist.

What Causes Bipolar Disorders?

"Depression is associated with a reduction of serotonin or norepinephrine transmitters. Conversely, a rapid increase of these chemicals may trigger mania."

—Jan Fawcett, Bernard Golden, and Nancy Rosenfeld, *New Hope for People with Bipolar Disorder*. New York: Three Rivers, 2007.

Fawcett is a professor of psychiatry at the University of New Mexico; Golden is a psychologist who practices in Chicago, Illinois; and Rosenfeld, a resident of Chicago, is a bipolar patient.

"Science has revealed clues as to why [hormonal] changes may occur in some women but further research is needed to definitively show what causes depression and mood disorders in women during hormonal transitions."

—Peter Schmidt, quoted in *Women's Health Weekly*, "Mental Health, Hormonal Changes and Depression: What Is the Connection?" November 29, 2007.

A physician, Schmidt is an investigator with the National Institute of Mental Health's Reproductive Endocrine Studies Unit.

* Editor's Note: While the definition of a primary source can be narrowly or broadly defined, for the purposes of Compact Research, a primary source consists of: 1) results of original research presented by an organization or researcher; 2) eyewitness accounts of events, personal experience, or work experience; 3) first-person editorials offering pundits' opinions; 4) government officials presenting political plans and/or policies; 5) representatives of organizations presenting testimony or policy.

" Dealing with mental illness and pregnancy was such a trial. But the first time I saw my daughter, I knew I'd do it all over again in a second. "

—Candace Watson, quoted in Michelle Roberts, "When Conception Is the Question," *BP*, Spring 2007. www.bphope.com.

Watson, a bipolar patient, lives in Alberta, Canada.

" In 1994, my mother committed suicide. My father was on a business trip when she drove the family van to a provincial park and attached a hose to the exhaust pipe, filling the car with carbon monoxide gas. . . . That's when Dad told me Mom's father had also committed suicide. "

—Autumn Stringam, "My New Ordinary Life," *Chatelaine*, May 2008.

A Canadian mother of four, Stringam wrote a memoir of bipolar disorder titled *A Promise of Hope*.

" The fascinating thing about bipolar disease in general . . . is that bipolar disease is heavily influenced by familial and therefore genetic inheritance. "

—Peter Whybrow, quoted in *Saturday Evening Post*, "Mood Swings: An Interview with Peter Whybrow," July/August 2005.

Whybrow is a professor of psychiatry at the University of California at Los Angeles.

" Our findings suggest that exposure to a harsh environment . . . may explain the relationship between childhood stressful events and a bipolar spectrum diagnosis. "

—Louisa D. Grandin, Lauren B. Alloy, and Lyn Y. Abramson, "Childhood Stressful Life Events and Bipolar Spectrum Disorder," *Journal of Social and Clinical Psychology*, April 2007.

Abramson, of the University of Wisconsin, and Grandin and Alloy of Temple University in Philadelphia, Pennsylvania, are psychologists who reported the results of a study in 2007 that concluded that children who grow up in environments of fear and violence have a greater likelihood of developing bipolar disorders.

❝In people who have bipolar disorder, sleep problems occur cyclically. They may fluctuate week to week or month to month. So in the manic or hypomanic phases, they get very little sleep but at times of depression, they may sleep or just stay in bed for excessive amounts of time.❞

—Michael J. Thorpy, quoted in Milly Dawson, "The Quest for Sleep," *BP*, Spring 2006. www.bphope.com.

Thorpy is director of the Sleep-Wake Disorder Center at Montefiore Medical Center in New York City.

❝I would promise things to people that I would do . . . but then I would shut down and forget all about them. When I would later remember what I had promised, I felt so guilty that I had failed.❞

—Cathy Denton, quoted in Michelle Roberts, "The Many Faces and Facets of BP," *BP*, Summer 2007. www.bphope.com.

Bipolar patient Denton lives in Maryville, Tennessee.

❝Like other mental illnesses, bipolar disorder cannot yet be identified physiologically—for example, through a blood test or a brain scan. Therefore, a diagnosis of bipolar disorder is made on the basis of symptoms, course of illness, and, when available, family history.❞

—National Institute of Mental Health, "Bipolar Disorder," January 2007. www.nimh.nih.gov.

The National Institute of Mental Health is the federal government's chief funding arm for research into mental illnesses.

❝A blood test to predict bipolar disorder? I don't think it will happen.❞

—Francis McMahon, quoted in Andy Coughlan, "Young and Moody or Mentally Ill?" *New Scientist*, May 19, 2007.

McMahon, a genetics scientist, is heading a project at the National Institutes of Health to identify common genes in bipolar patients.

❝We need to be able to tell people, before they have mania, that they have bipolar.❞

—Gin Malhi, quoted in Daniel Williams, "Light in the Dark," *Time International*, April 9, 2007.

Malhi is director of psychological medicine at Royal North Shore Hospital in Sydney, Australia.

❝Most of our current understanding of bipolar disorder is based on properties of patients experiencing depressive or manic syndromes; too little information is available on what predisposes people to these episodes and on the factors that determine the cause of illness.❞

—Allan C. Swann, "What Is Bipolar Disorder?" *American Journal of Psychiatry*, February 2006.

Swann is a professor of psychiatry at the University of Texas.

What Causes Bipolar Disorders?

- If one identical twin is bipolar, the other twin has a **65 percent** chance of also being bipolar.

- More than **66 percent** of bipolar patients have at least one close relative who is also either bipolar or suffers from depression.

- A Massachusetts study found that portions of the frontal lobes in 39 bipolar patients were as much as **9 percent** smaller than patients in a control group.

- According to a three-month California study, **65 percent** of the female bipolar patients reported significant mood swings as they were menstruating.

- A Danish study found that children born to fathers who are over the age of 55 are **37 percent** more likely to develop bipolar disorders than children born to men in their 20s.

- Bipolar patients have a three times greater-than-average chance of developing **autoimmune thyroid disease**, in which the body's immune system attacks the thyroid gland.

- An Arizona study reported that **12 of 17** bipolar women who went through childbirth experienced postpartum depression after their babies were born.

The Hypothalamus-Pituitary Axis Could Trigger Bipolar Episodes

Adrenaline is a hormone that enables the body to react to stress. The hypothalamus and pituitary gland work together to govern the release of the hormone. If the hypothalamus-pituitary axis malfunctions, too much or too little adrenaline can be released into the body. In bipolar patients, an oversecretion of adrenaline usually results in an episode of mania while too little adrenaline can result in depression.

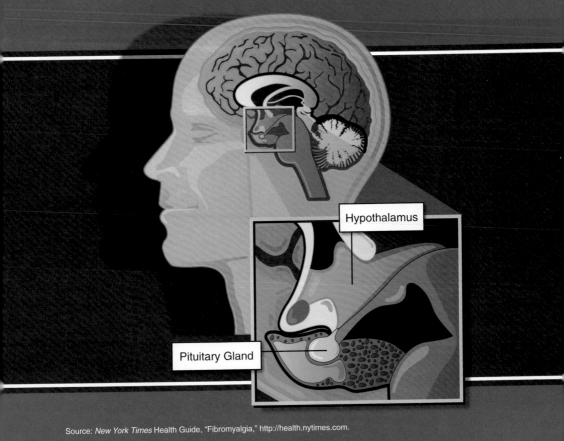

Hypothalamus

Pituitary Gland

Source: *New York Times* Health Guide, "Fibromyalgia," http://health.nytimes.com.

- Bipolar patients may share as many as 80 common genes, 8 of which affect how the brain responds to **neurotransmitters**.

- Harvard and Emory universities found that bipolar women who stop taking their mood stabilizing drugs during pregnancy spent **40 percent** of their pregnancies in the throes of depression or mania; women who continued to take their medications during their pregnancies spent just **8 percent** of their pregnancies with bipolar symptoms.

Brain Malfunction in a Bipolar Patient

Two components of the brain affected by bipolar disorders are the hippocampus and amygdalae. Bipolar disorder causes the hippocampus, which stores memories, to shrink in size. The amygdalae, which are two almond-sized balls of tissue near the ears, control judgment and help the body react to stressful situations. In bipolar patients, the amygdalae often misfire, causing the patient to overreact to stressful situations.

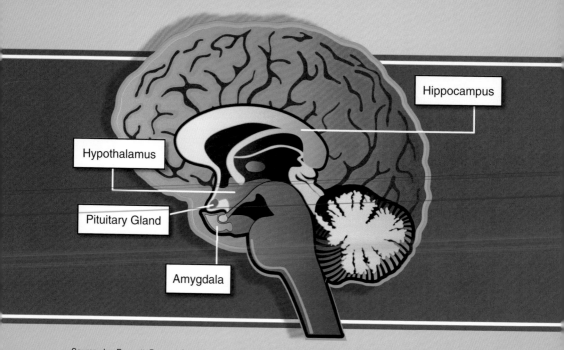

Source: Jan Fawcett, Bernard Golden, and Nancy Rosefeld, *New Hope for People with Bipolar Disorder*. New York: Three Rivers, 2007, p. 49.

Bipolar Patients Often Need Very Little Sleep

The suprachiasmatic nucleus, or SCN, is found in the hypothalamus. The SCN regulates a person's circadian rhythms, telling him or her when to go to bed at night and rise in the morning. In a bipolar patient, the SCN often malfunctions, throwing off the patient's biological clock. That is why bipolar patients seem to need very little sleep in their manic phases.

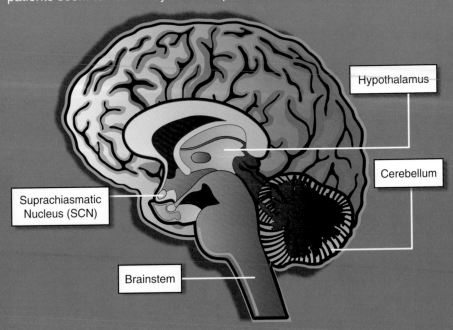

Source: Harvard University School of Medicine, "Under the Brain's Control," http://healthysleep.med.harvard.edu.

- **Thirty-three percent** of bipolar patients have at least one bipolar parent.

- Bipolar patients who experience a **traumatic event** in their lives take three times longer to recover from their symptoms than other bipolar patients.

- A baby whose mother takes lithium during pregnancy has a **1 in 1,000** chance of developing a defective heart valve; the risk of developing a defective heart valve among all American babies is **1 in 20,000**.

How the Thyroid Gland Affects Bipolar Patients

The thyroid gland produces hormones that regulate the body's energy. Bipolar patients suffer from the condition known as hyperthyroidism, in which the body produces too much energy, and hypothyroidism, in which too little energy is manufactured. In bipolar patients, hyperthyroidism can lead to manic episodes while hypothyroidism can result in depressive moods. Meanwhile, in bipolar patients the pituitary gland often produces an imbalance of adrenaline, sparking episodes of depression and mania.

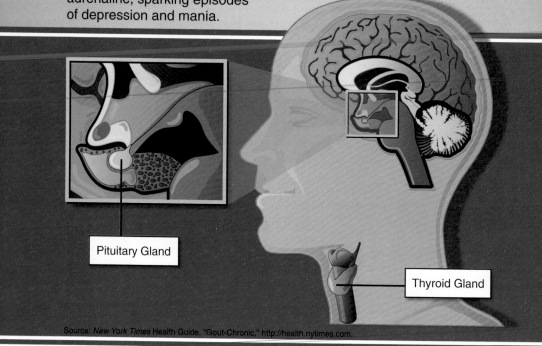

Pituitary Gland

Thyroid Gland

Source: *New York Times* Health Guide, "Gout-Chronic," http://health.nytimes.com.

- A Canadian study found that bipolar teens often secrete high levels of the hormone **cortisol** in the mid-afternoon, explaining why many of them enter manic phases as they get out of school.

- In a Texas study, scientists were able to induce periods of mania in laboratory mice by disrupting their **circadian rhythms**.

- According to a Massachusetts study, bipolar mothers who nurse their babies do not pass along dangerous levels of lithium in their **breast milk**.

How Do Bipolar Disorders Affect People?

66 When I'm depressed I feel extremely blank. I want to sleep all the time and have a sincere desire to die. I feel lots of pain as if I have the flu . . . and I have no desire to eat. I also experience paranoia, delusional thinking, and have gone through periods of cutting myself. Basically, I feel like the walking dead. 99

—Laurel Powell, a massage therapist and bipolar patient from Medford, Oregon.

The Nightmare of Bipolar Disorders

Bipolar disorders can be devastating to patients as well as to their families and friends. Bipolar patients find themselves enduring long fits of depression, angry and violent behavior, substance abuse, and other risky behaviors. In many cases, the stresses they feel in their lives spark their bipolar episodes.

For bipolar patients, life is never easy. As they deal with their mood swings, they miss a lot of school and work. In their depressive phases, they may not be able to rise from their beds in the morning. In their manic phases, they may stay up all night, engage in impulsive sexual relationships, or go on spending sprees.

They often disappoint friends, family members, and coworkers, who may be relying on them. Says Jan Fawcett, a New Mexico psychiatrist and author, "When someone whose spouse is in a manic episode and refuses treatment asks me what he or she can do, I tell them to close the bank account and wait it out."[33]

Stress on Families

When Erica Poole was a young girl, her father told her a secret about her mother—she had a bipolar disorder. At the time, Erica was too young to understand what that meant, but she did agree with her father's description of her mother—that her sadness would often last for months, but those periods were occasionally interrupted by brief episodes of hyperactivity and excitement. "We definitely noticed that our mom had very extreme moods,"[34] says Erica.

By the time Erica turned 16, she realized just how deeply troubled her mother had become. Her mother's depressive episodes would usually last all winter. At other times of the year, her mania took over. According to Erica, her mother's episodes of mania were not entirely disagreeable— she would plan and carry out elaborate parties for the children.

At other times, though, Erica's mother would turn mean. "The bad side of her being manic was that she'd be irritable and say mean things," says Erica. "She imitated me in a whiny voice, like a bratty sib would do, which is totally weird coming from your mom. She didn't mean to hurt me, but it did. When winter came the parties would stop and she'd just lie in the dark."[35]

> In their depressive phases, they may not be able to rise from their beds in the morning. In their manic phases, they may stay up all night, engage in impulsive sexual relationships, or go on spending sprees.

At first, Erica responded to her mother's moodiness with anger. When her mother would get irritable and snap at her, Erica responded by snapping back. Eventually, Erica learned to ignore her mother's tirades. In fact, she tried to avoid her mother at home, throwing herself into schoolwork or other activities. Erica's brother had a harder time accepting his mother's condition, continuing to argue with her even though the constant bickering never seemed to resolve anything.

Fortunately, Erica's father could be counted on to step in and calm everyone down. Whenever Erica's mother seemed to be in a depressive or irritable mood, her father would take the children away, perhaps for dinner by themselves, until things calmed down at home. Eventually, the doctor was able to adjust her mother's medication so that she gained a measure of control over her mood swings.

Economic Impact

Certainly, there is an emotional burden on families of bipolar patients, but there is also an economic burden. Drugs, psychiatric care, and other costs are expensive, often totaling tens of thousands of dollars a year. Many families who are covered by health insurance are fortunate because most of the costs are paid by insurers. But for families with no insurance or limited insurance, the costs can be staggering.

A study published by the American Psychiatric Association journal *Psychiatric Services* found that the annual treatment cost for a bipolar patient runs about $19,000 a year. And not all of that is attributable to the costs of mood stabilizing drugs and psychotherapy. Often, bipolar patients require treatment for physical ailments. Many must receive treatment for their drug and alcohol addictions. Many bipolar patients try to commit suicide. If they fail they may severely injure themselves, which means they may need to be treated in hospital emergency rooms and admitted to hospitals as they recover.

A separate study published by *Psychiatric Services* estimated that bipolar patients average health-care bills that are four times higher than people who do not suffer from the disorder. Overall, the study said, bipolar disorders cost the American economy as much as $44 billion a year.

Costs to Society

A lot of the economic burden of bipolar disorders occurs in the workplace. When bipolar employees are in their depressive phases, they may not feel well enough to show up for work. If they are in their manic phases, they may be very hard workers—if they show up for work. Indeed, it is not unusual for an employee in a manic phase to forget all about work and instead follow an impulse to do something else that day. In the meantime, coworkers have to pick up the slack, or employers must bring in temporary workers to do the job. It all means that the employers of bipolar

> " There is an emotional burden on families of bipolar patients but there is also an economic burden. Drugs, psychiatric care, and other costs are expensive, often totaling tens of thousands of dollars a year. "

patients have to make expenditures they would not ordinarily have to make for employees who do not suffer from the disorder.

Terri Cheney, the California attorney and bipolar patient, recalled having a very difficult time dealing with the pressures of the workplace. In fact, Cheney left a very large Los Angeles law firm for a smaller firm, hoping the pressures would abate. They did not. Arriving for work one day, Cheney recalls:

Message slips were cascading off my chair to the floor. I picked one up: "Notice of appeal." I picked up a few more. "Urgent." "Appeal." "Call immediately." I swept the rest of the slips off my chair, sat down, and put my head on my desk. The lights kept blinking, the phone kept ringing, but I couldn't move my hand to pick it up. I knew it wouldn't make the noise go away. It would never go away. It would only be followed by the next noise, which might even be louder. Better just to sit there, quietly, my head on my desk, until it was time to go home.[36]

Substance Abuse

Certainly, one of the reasons for so much missed time at work by bipolar patients is chronic substance abuse, which has ruined the careers and futures of many sufferers of the disorder. Actress Margot Kidder shot to fame when she portrayed Lois Lane in the 1978 film version of *Superman* as well as its two sequels. Kidder kept up a busy schedule as an actress even though she had been experiencing the mood swings common among bipolar patients. To cope, she turned to cocaine and alcohol.

For Kidder, her substance abuse served only to enhance her mood swings. In 1996 she disappeared from her California home. Police found her a few days later, dirty and disoriented, wandering aimlessly through backyards in an upscale Los Angeles neighborhood. She spent a brief time in a mental hospital and was then released. Although Kidder has shaken off her addictions, she has acted only occasionally since that episode.

Another bipolar woman who turned to alcohol and drugs was Carrie Fisher, best known for her role as Princess Leia in the 1977 film *Star Wars* and its two sequels. Fisher grew up in Hollywood—her mother is singer and actress Debbie Reynolds. Fisher herself started performing at the age of 12. But there was a dark side to her glitzy world. As a young girl, Fisher started experiencing bipolar symptoms.

As the *Star Wars* films evolved into big box-office hits, Fisher turned to alcohol, cocaine, and the prescription painkiller Percodan. In 1985 she was hospitalized after a drug overdose. Eventually, her career ground to a halt as she found herself dealing with the dual burdens of bipolar disorder and substance abuse. She said: "I used to think I was a drug addict, pure and simple—just someone who could not stop taking drugs willfully. And I was that. But it turns out that I am severely manic depressive. I outlasted my problems. I am mentally ill. I can say that. I am not ashamed of that. I'm still surviving it."[37]

> " Many bipolar patients try to commit suicide. If they fail they may severely injure themselves, which means they may need to be treated in hospital emergency rooms and admitted to hospitals as they recover. "

Physical Illnesses

Substance abuse often leads to physical illnesses, including heart and liver diseases caused by heavy drinking. Excessive marijuana use can lead to memory loss and other brain damage. There are also growing indications that smoking marijuana is far more harmful to the lungs and other organs of the body than cigarette smoking.

Cigarette smoking is very common among bipolar patients—a 2008 study by the University of Melbourne in Australia found that more than half of the 800 bipolar patients who participated in the research project were cigarette smokers. Indeed, many bipolar patients rely heavily on cigarettes, using them as a crutch during their depressive phases and savoring the nicotine rush that smoking provides during their manic episodes. Of course, the health effects of cigarette smoking have been well documented for years—cancer, heart disease, and the lung disease emphysema are all possible outcomes of tobacco use.

Going Off Their Medication

Bipolar patients often display symptoms of a condition known as anosognosia, which is a disbelief in their diagnoses. In other words, they do not believe they are ill. Mostly, anosognosia manifests itself in the manic phase of the disorder. When bipolar patients are feeling good about themselves, they often stop taking their medications. It is estimated that about half of all bipolar patients stop taking their drugs at some point in their therapies.

> It is not unusual for an employee in a manic phase to forget all about work and instead follow an impulse to do something else that day.

"The hard thing about bipolar disorder is that you have intervals of normalcy," says Donna Thomas, a bipolar patient from Conestoga, Pennsylvania. "If you have a headache, for example, and the pain goes away, you stop taking medicine. So I stopped taking my medicine . . . I believed the same thing that other people believed that if you pick yourself up, work hard enough and try hard enough, that you can get past the need for medicine."[38]

Some bipolar patients also go off their medication because lithium and other drugs prescribed for manic depression can have side effects. Indeed, side effects for lithium include headache, nausea, vomiting, diarrhea, drowsiness, lack of coordination, loss of appetite, muscle weakness, slurred speech, and trembling. Some bipolar patients find themselves trying to make their way through life in a drugged daze. Marya Hornbacher said that soon after her doctor changed her medication, she became so drugged that she stayed in bed for two weeks, spending most of the time asleep. When she finally summoned the strength to get out of bed, Hornbacher said:

My head feels like it's wrapped in cotton batting and weighs a ton. I'm clearly drugged. I have no idea what day it is, or even what season of the year. . . . I crawl out of bed, unsteady on my legs. I make my way down the hallway, holding on to the wall. I wander into the kitchen and stand there in my gross pajamas, weak, filthy, hungry, cold.[39]

Eventually, most bipolar patients do report their side effects to their doctors, who can help them overcome the nausea, headaches, and other symptoms by altering their doses. Also, many bipolar patients do come to realize that if they go off their medication, their mood swings will return. Says TV actor and bipolar patient Maurice Benard, "The only side effect [of my medication] is, if I don't take it, I have a breakdown."[40]

Risky Behavior

A lot of what goes wrong in a bipolar person's life occurs during the manic phase of the illness—a time when the patient feels he or she can do no wrong. During the manic phase, the patient feels an overwhelming sense of euphoria, extreme optimism, inflated self-esteem, racing thoughts, aggressive behavior, and an inability to concentrate. All of these factors could lead the patient to make poor decisions. In many cases, bipolar patients go on spending sprees, spending hundreds or thousands of dollars on ill-advised purchases. Many bipolar patients become promiscuous, launching into impulsive relationships with strangers.

Terri Cheney recalled going through a manic episode in which she had not slept for three days. During the episode, she went grocery shopping. At the supermarket, she encountered a man named Jeff. She found herself attracted to Jeff, and engaged him in a wordy conversation in which she talked about herself and her interests and ques-

> " [Margot] Kidder kept up a busy schedule as an actress even though she had been experiencing the mood swings common among bipolar patients. To cope, she turned to cocaine and alcohol. "

tioned him about his life. Completely on impulse, she made a date with Jeff. Returning home, she suddenly felt depression come on. Leaving her groceries unpacked, Cheney fell into bed and remained there for the next two days.

She woke up to the sound of a ringing phone. It was now Saturday afternoon, and the caller was Jeff. He wanted to know if she was ready for their date. Cheney barely remembered meeting him. Later, when Jeff picked her up, she was still in the throes of a depressive episode and said little as she greeted him. "I had nothing to say, not then or at dinner," she says. "So Jeff talked, a lot at first, then less and less until finally, during dessert, he asked, 'You don't by any chance have a twin, do you?'"[41]

> **Many bipolar patients rely heavily on cigarettes, using them as a crutch during their depressive phases and savoring the nicotine rush that smoking provides during their manic episodes.**

That unhappy date was not even the end of the relationship—a few weeks later, Cheney was again in a manic phase. She called Jeff and invited him over for dinner. On the day of the dinner, still in a manic phase, she spent hours cleaning her apartment, cooking the dinner, and agonizing over what to wear, finally picking a sexy cocktail dress. And then, just a few minutes before Jeff arrived, she lapsed into a deep depression. She crawled into bed and, moments later, refused to answer the doorbell.

Suicide and Bipolar Patients

Bipolar patients have some of the highest rates of suicide among patients with mental illnesses—as high as 15 percent. Still, friends and family members of bipolar patients are often shocked at the news of a loved one's suicide.

Software millionaire Steve Thomas was diagnosed with bipolar disorder but refused treatment. Living in Hawaii, Thomas began displaying more and more impulsive and outrageous behaviors—he once attacked a police officer. On June 30, 2008, Thomas disappeared. Police searched for the missing man, finally finding his body about 2 weeks later at the bottom of a 200-foot cliff (61m) near Honolulu. Authorities concluded that Thomas had jumped to his death. Months before, Thomas's father, Ralph, spent some time with his son. "I asked him if he was ever thinking of injuring himself, and he said no," Ralph Thomas said. "It's mind-boggling how quickly it turned around. He was always the one we didn't have to worry about. He had everything."[42]

Steve Thomas left behind grieving friends and family members, who wondered what more they could have done to prevent his tragic death. For friends, family members, and coworkers who find themselves enduring the mood swings and outrageous behaviors of bipolar patients, life can often be frustrating. Imagine the surprise of Terri Cheney's would-be boyfriend when a far different person than the woman he met in the produce aisle showed up for dinner and, later, would not even answer the doorbell. But there are also many people who understand the plight of bipolar patients—people like Erica Poole and her father, who found ways to support Erica's mother through her bipolar episodes. Other bipolar patients, who may not receive such strong support at home, often find their careers and lives cut short.

Primary Source Quotes*

How Do Bipolar Disorders Affect People?

66 If you have a parent who is bipolar, you can tough it out like I did. Honestly, it will make you stronger and more compassionate. It hasn't been easy, but I definitely feel I've become a better person for having gone through it. 99

—Erica Poole, quoted in Sandy Fertman Ryan, "Stranger in My House," *Girls' Life*, February 2006.

Poole, 16, learned to endure her mother's manic depressive episodes.

66 Bipolar people don't recognize when they're having a manic episode, but their family members and friends, who are often the targets of these episodes, do. 99

—Igor Galynker, quoted in Marrecca Fiore, "New Medications More Effective for Treating Bipolar Disorder," Fox News, October 10, 2007. www.foxnews.com.

Galynker is director of the Family Center for Bipolar Disorder at Beth Israel Medical Center in New York City.

* Editor's Note: While the definition of a primary source can be narrowly or broadly defined, for the purposes of Compact Research, a primary source consists of: 1) results of original research presented by an organization or researcher; 2) eyewitness accounts of events, personal experience, or work experience; 3) first-person editorials offering pundits' opinions; 4) government officials presenting political plans and/or policies; 5) representatives of organizations presenting testimony or policy.

"Bipolar disorder has a clear economic impact on patients with the disorder, their families, caregivers, and society as a whole."

—Glen L. Stimmel, "The Economic Burden of Bipolar Disorder," *Psychiatric Services*, February 2004.

Stimmel, a professor at the University of Southern California, is the author of a study on the economic impacts of bipolar disorders.

....

"The fact that patients with bipolar disorder incurred more than four times the health care charges of the average [worker] speaks to the need for innovative and creative programs to manage this population."

—Russell L. Knoth, Kristina Chen, and Eskinder Tafesse, "Costs Associated with the Treatment of Patients with Bipolar Disorder in a Managed Care Organization," *Psychiatric Services*, December 2004.

Knoth, Chen, and Tafesse headed a study that examined the health-care costs of bipolar workers.

....

"If you have a genetic vulnerability to bipolar illness, any drug abuse ... not only brings it on earlier, it worsens its course and makes it (harder) to treat."

—Kay Redfield Jamison, quoted in Joe Saraceno, "A Troubled Life on the Line," *USA Today*, February 3, 2005.

Jamison is a professor of psychology at Johns Hopkins University in Baltimore, Maryland.

....

"The ramifications of bipolar disorder include a significant economic toll, as well as family disruption, caregiver stress, and an individual burden encompassing [other] illnesses, substance abuse, poor functionality, and high suicide risk."

—National Alliance on Mental Illness, "The Impact and Cost of Mental Illness: The Case of Bipolar Disorder," 2008. www.nami.org.

The National Alliance on Mental Illness is a support group for mentally ill patients and their families.

....

❝ I've had an awful lot of highs and they were great. But the price I've paid for them is pretty tough to accept and . . . I can't pay that price anymore. ❞

— Margot Kidder, quoted in Lauren Cahoon, Radha Chitale, and Aina Hunter, "The Cost of Creativity: Bipolar Disorder and the Stars," ABC News, March 21, 2008. http://abcnews.go.com.

Kidder, a bipolar patient, saw her film career cut short due to drug and alcohol abuse.

❝ For bipolar and depressive disorders, patients may benefit from being specifically counselled on the importance of addressing smoking as part of their mood disorder management. ❞

—Felicity Ng, quoted in Andrew Czyzewski, "Smoking Interferes with Treatment for Bipolar Mania," MedWire News, August 1, 2008. www.medwire-news.md.

Ng conducted a study at the University of Melbourne in Australia on smoking habits among bipolar patients.

❝ This work confirms that bipolar disorder in adolescents is a huge risk factor for smoking and substance abuse. ❞

—Timothy Willens, quoted in *Science Daily*, "Increased Risk of Smoking, Substance Abuse in Bipolar Adolescents Confirmed," June 4, 2008. www.sciencedaily.com.

Willens, director of substance abuse services at Massachusetts General Hospital, headed a study that explored smoking and substance abuse in bipolar teenagers.

66 The medical burden in bipolar disorder is associated with a clustering of risk factors—obesity, smoking, unhealthy dietary habits—and inadequate utilization of preventative and primary healthcare. 99

—Roger S. McIntyre et al., "Bipolar Disorder and Diabetes Mellitus: Epidemiology, Etiology, and Treatment Implications," *Annual Review of Clinical Psychology*, April–June 2005. www.ncbi.nlm.nih.gov.

The authors conducted a study focusing on the relationship between bipolar disorders and diabetes for United Health Network of Toronto, Canada.

66 I learned that the manic side of the manic depressive combo is, weirdly, linked to a shopping impulse. . . . I did have a robust hunting-and-gathering impulse. [My husband] marveled at the service I provided local merchants that spring, mopping up their excess merchandise. 99

—Jane Pauley, "An Excerpt from *Skywriting: A Life Out of the Blue*," *Saturday Evening Post*, March/April 2007.

Pauley, a TV journalist, is a bipolar patient and the author of *Skywriting: A Life Out of the Blue*.

66 I tried to commit suicide by ingesting handfuls of my prescribed antidepressant. In the following six months, I had several hospitalizations as my symptoms would come and go with no reason. Because I had tried to commit suicide, I was committed to the 'Big House'—the state psychiatric hospital. 99

—Brian Marshall, quoted in Michelle Roberts, "The Many Faces and Facets of BP," *BP*, Summer 2007. www.bphope.com.

Bipolar patient Marshall is a journalist who lives near Detroit, Michigan.

How Do Bipolar Disorders Affect People?

- A total of **21 percent** of bipolar patients suffer from diabetes, a rate that is 10 times greater than what is found in the general population.

- **Twenty-nine percent** of bipolar patients suffer from high blood pressure, a rate that is 16 times greater than normal.

- An Israeli study found that **43 percent** of bipolar teenagers in Israel smoke cigarettes, a rate that is **16 percent** higher than the general population of the country.

- **Fifty-eight percent** of bipolar participants in a University of Melbourne study were smokers.

- A Belgian study in 2008 found that **7 percent** of bipolar patients are diabetic; another **23 percent** of the patients suffered from a prediabetic condition, meaning their blood sugar levels were particularly high.

- A Massachusetts study reported that **34 percent** of bipolar teens admitted to abusing drugs and alcohol, a rate **30 percent** higher than the control group.

- **Forty-four percent** of bipolar patients who abuse alcohol also abuse drugs.

- A Canadian study reported that **25 percent** of bipolar patients attempt suicide at least once in their lifetimes.

Employer Costs of Bipolar Disorders

Harvard University Medical School compared the costs employers bear for hiring bipolar patients with those of hiring patients who suffer from depression only. The study found that bipolar patients miss more that twice as much work as depressed patients. Also, bipolar patients cost their employers nearly $10,000 a year in lost productivity while depressed patients cost their employers about half that.

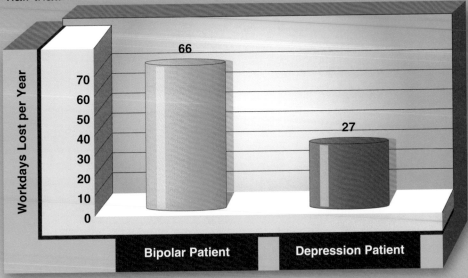

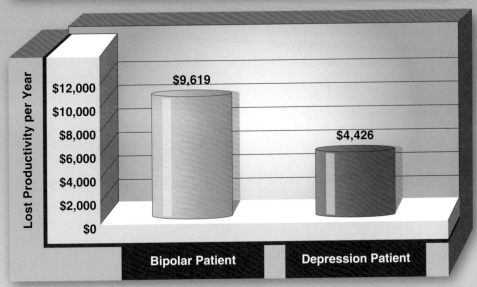

Source: Ronald C. Kessler et al., "Prevalence and Effects of Mood Disorders on Work Performance in a Nationally Representative Sample of U.S. Workers," *American Journal of Psychiatry*, September 2006.

Mental Disorders Are Responsible for Many Teenage Suicides

Researchers for the World Health Organization and the Christchurch School of Medicine in New Zealand reviewed 894 cases of teenage suicide in which the patients had been diagnosed with mental illnesses or had acknowledged abusing drugs and alcohol before their deaths. In 42 percent of the cases, the research revealed that the patients had been diagnosed with mood disorders, including bipolar disorders and depression. The remaining teenagers were drug and alcohol abusers or patients diagnosed with disruptive disorders, such as attention deficit hyperactivity disorder. The researchers also said the figures indicate there is some overlap in the statistics, which explains why the numbers add up to more than 100 percent; it is likely that some bipolar patients were also substance abusers.

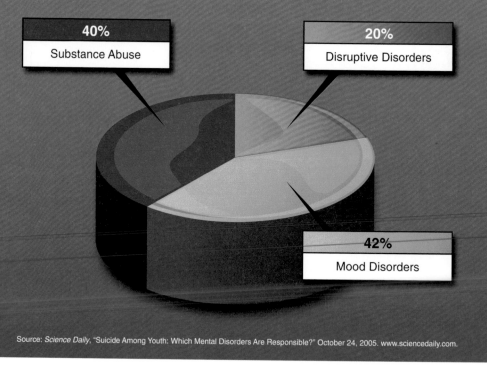

40%
Substance Abuse

20%
Disruptive Disorders

42%
Mood Disorders

Source: *Science Daily*, "Suicide Among Youth: Which Mental Disorders Are Responsible?" October 24, 2005. www.sciencedaily.com.

- **Thirty-nine percent** of bipolar patients who abuse drugs and alcohol attempt to take their own lives.

Substance Abuse Among Bipolar Teens

A study by Massachusetts General Hospital concluded that 34 percent of bipolar teens abuse alcohol or drugs or smoke cigarettes, while just 4 percent of nonbipolar teens abuse substances. Nearly a quarter of the bipolar teens drink, use drugs, or smoke cigarettes, while 14 percent are regarded as drug dependent. The 2008 study followed the habits of 105 bipolar teens and 98 teens who had not been diagnosed as bipolar.

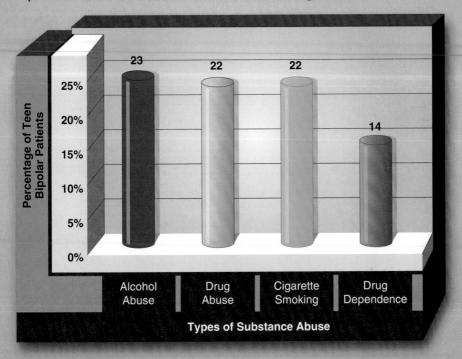

Sources: *Science Daily*, "Increased Risk of Smoking, Substance Abuse In Bipolar Adolescents Confirmed," June 4, 2008. www.sciencedaily.com; Marlene Busko, "Huge Risk of Substance Abuse Found Among Teens with Bipolar Disorder," *Medscape*, July 2, 2008. www.medscape.com.

- About **33 percent** of bipolar patients who participated in a University of Pittsburgh study were obese.

- In a Seattle, Washington, study, bipolar patients composed **5 percent** of the mentally ill clients in the region, yet they required **40 percent** of the cost of mental health and substance abuse services.

- The average health-care bills for bipolar patients are **400 percent** greater than for people who do not suffer from the disorder.

- Life expectancy for a bipolar patient is **69**, which is **9 years less** than the average life expectancy for all Americans.

Some Bipolar Patients Think About Suicide

Authors of a study published in the journal *Suicide and Life-Threatening Behavior* interviewed bipolar patients who admitted to be contemplating suicide. By interviewing the patients, the authors were able to determine that their average age is 41 and the majority are females. In addition, the authors found that most of the patients are unemployed and living alone, and that most hold a high school degree only or did not finish high school. Seventy-nine percent earned less than $30,000 a year.

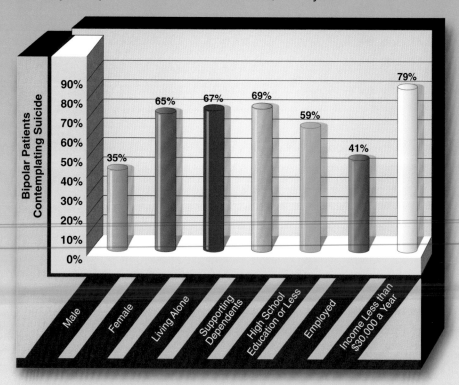

Source: Michael H. Allen et al., "Contributors to Suicidal Ideation Among Bipolar Patients with and Without a History of Suicide Attempts," *Suicide and Life-Threatening Behavior*, December 2005.

What Treatments Are Available for Bipolar Disorders?

66 **The shame is in having a mental illness and not facing it and getting it treated, because you're going to destroy your life and probably destroy your marriage and probably destroy friendships. You're probably going to disappoint people; you're probably going to have trouble keeping your job.** 99

—Margaret Trudeau, bipolar patient and former first lady of Canada.

There Is No Cure

When a patient is diagnosed with a bipolar disorder and accepts the diagnosis, he or she must also accept the hard truth about the illness: There is no cure. Bipolar disorder is a mental illness that the patient will have to endure for the rest of his or her life. The best hope for the patient is to find the right combination of mood stabilizing drugs, psychotherapy, and other treatments that will help him or her successfully manage the symptoms, which can be extremely unpredictable.

The good news, though, is that there are drugs that have proved to be very effective in managing bipolar symptoms. Other therapies, including psychiatric counseling, cognitive behavioral therapy, and lifestyle changes, can help reduce the frequency and severity of bipolar episodes. Says California psychiatrist and author Wes Burgess: "With successful treatment, people with bipolar disorder are healthy and can achieve the kind of life they want and deserve. For the first time in history, we have a broad choice of effective treatments for bipolar disorder."[43]

Indeed, mental health professionals have a far greater understanding of the disease than they had some 30 years ago, when the illness known as manic depression was renamed bipolar disorder. Now, in addition to treating the illness with drugs and psychotherapy, they understand the importance of creating healthy environments for the patients and involving family members in the treatments of their loved ones.

Saving Lives Through Better Diagnoses

A main problem with treating a bipolar disorder is diagnosing it early enough so the patient can benefit from the therapies. If the psychiatrist fails to recognize the symptoms of bipolar disorder, it is likely the physician will prescribe an antidepressant drug such as Prozac. In bipolar patients, antidepressants often do more harm than good. Typically, antidepressants step up the production of the neurotransmitter serotonin, which can enhance the feeling of euphoria in the patient. However, in bipolar patients, antidepressants often speed up the occurrence of the patient's manic episodes, which are then followed by more frequent depressive episodes. In other words, instead of eliminating the patient's depression, antidepressant drugs tend to trigger more depressive episodes. Misdiagnosing bipolar disorder and prescribing the wrong drug can have a disastrous effect on the patient.

Many times, bipolar patients commit suicide before they have been correctly diagnosed.

> " Instead of eliminating the [bipolar] patient's depression, antidepressant drugs tend to trigger more depressive episodes. "

Today, psychiatrists are more familiar with bipolar symptoms. While they are interviewing the depressed patient for the first time, they may ask many questions about the length and severity of the depressive episodes as well as how the patient acts when not depressed. Does he or she stay up all night? Is the patient promiscuous? Does the patient go on impulsive spending sprees? The psychiatrist will also ask a lot of questions about family history, seeking a genetic link between the patient and relatives who may have been bipolar.

Psychiatrists must diagnose bipolar disorders without the benefit of physical evidence. That may soon change. Using magnetic resonance imaging, or MRI, physicians are developing techniques for photographing the brains of manic depressive patients. By using MRI technology they can observe the subtle differences that serve as identifiers for bipolar disorders.

MRI tests utilize magnets that energize certain atoms in human cells. During the test, the scanner broadcasts radio waves through the body that strike the energized cells, producing an image. When producing a scan of a bipolar patient's brain, the MRI can detect the concentration of chemicals in the brain, signifying the chemical imbalances that cause bipolar symptoms. Also, the MRI can provide images of the tissue loss in the brain caused by bipolar disorders.

> " Using magnetic resonance imaging, or MRI, physicians are developing techniques for photographing the brains of manic depressive patients. "

"[In 2005], there were 30,000 suicides among depressed people, who may never have had the diagnosis of bipolar because they had not yet experienced the manic phase of the disease," says radiologist John D. Port, who has performed brains scans on bipolar patients at the Mayo Clinic in Rochester, Minnesota. "Clearly, if we could develop an imaging tool . . . to objectively diagnose bipolar disease, much of this morbidity and mortality could be avoided."[44] Currently, just a handful of hospitals are able to detect bipolar disorders through MRI brain scanning, but the technology is expected to gain wider use in the future.

Mood Stabilizers

Once the bipolar patient is diagnosed, it is likely the doctor will prescribe mood stabilizing drugs. Lithium is the oldest and most frequently prescribed drug for bipolar patients. The effectiveness of lithium on manic depression was first discovered in 1948 by Australian psychiatrist John Cade, who found that it had a calming effect on laboratory animals. Human tests soon confirmed that lithium could control the manic episodes of bipolar patients. By the 1970s, lithium had gained widespread use for manic depression.

Lithium can effectively control the neurotransmitter glutamate. If too much glutamate is released by the brain, manic episodes often occur. If too little glutamate is released, depressive episodes are often the result. Lithium is able to restore a balance to the flow of glutamate released by the brain.

However, the drug is not perfect. Many patients develop a resistance to lithium, and it is often necessary for them to have their doses adjusted after they start exhibiting symptoms again. In addition, doctors often find they have to prescribe supplemental drugs to patients, particularly those who need extra help controlling their depressive symptoms. The drug lamotrigine is often prescribed as a supplemental drug for patients on lithium. The drug was first prescribed to epilepsy patients to help reduce their seizures. It was also found to delay the onset of depressive episodes in bipolar patients, and now it is frequently part of a bipolar patient's therapy.

John Nurnberger Jr., director of psychiatric research at Indiana University School of Medicine, believes lamotrigine is so effective that it could probably be used in place of lithium. He points out that the drug does not carry as many harsh side effects as lithium, which means bipolar patients may be less likely to stop taking it. "The side effect profile is very favorable," he says. "It is easier to take than lithium."[45]

> " Bipolar patients learn very early in their therapies that if they fail to stick to their drug regimens, their mood swings will return. "

Other new drugs that cause fewer side effects than lithium are among a class of antipsychotic medications that regulate the neurotransmitters dopamine and serotonin. The drugs reduce the amount of dopamine, which cuts down on the amount of hormones released during manic episodes, while at the same time enhancing the flow of serotonin, which improves mood.

In the past, the drugs were employed to treat schizophrenia and other psychotic illnesses in which patients lose touch with reality, but doctors have found they have a high success rate among bipolar patients. "They were repurposed for use in bipolar disorder because of the overall tranquilizing effect that they have," says Massachusetts psychiatrist Keith Ablow. "Some people with bipolar disorder also suffer psychotic symptoms during the manic phase where they are delusional or hear voices or see visions. These drugs can be used also to control those symptoms."[46] The antipsychotic drugs do carry side effects—such as weight gain, sluggishness and nausea—but they are regarded as less severe than lithium.

Other drugs that may be prescribed to bipolar patients are calcium channel blockers, which are typically prescribed to patients suffering from high blood pressure. (Blood vessels clogged by calcium deposits are often a cause of hypertension.) Since calcium buildup on neurons is believed to be a cause of manic episodes, calcium blocking drugs may help bipolar patients control their symptoms.

> **Regarded as an important component of treatment for bipolar disorders, psychotherapy helps patients gain an insight into their moods, helping them keep sadness and euphoria in perspective.**

Some of the most severe cases of bipolar disorder do not react to drugs. In those cases, much more radical therapy may be employed. Some bipolar patients undergo electroconvulsive therapy, or ECT, also known as electroshock therapy. In ECT the brain receives a jolt of electricity. TV talk show host Dick Cavett endured years of bipolar symptoms that never responded to drug therapy. Finally, he consented to ECT. "In my case, electroconvulsive therapy was miraculous," he said. "My wife was dubious, but when she came into the room afterward, I sat up and said, 'Look who's back among the living.' It was like a magic wand."[47]

ECT triggers a convulsion that alters the chemistry in the brain. In most cases, patients undergo about 9 or 12 electroconvulsive treatments, but in some cases patients have to undergo occasional treatments for the rest of their lives. Says Detroit, Michigan, psychiatrist C. Edward Coffey:

> I have dozens of people like that who get it for years and years—as does every practitioner in the country. With people who don't respond to medications you have to

administer ECT for the rest of their life. The rule in the field is that what got you well, keeps you well. If a patient's depression is one that requires lifetime treatment with ECT, then ECT would be used for life.[48]

Benefits of Psychotherapy

Bipolar patients must do more than just take drugs to stabilize their moods. Regarded as an important component of treatment for bipolar disorders, psychotherapy helps patients gain an insight into their moods, helping them keep sadness and euphoria in perspective. Under the care of a psychiatrist, patients can explore their emotions and find ways in which they can control their behaviors. In many cases, psychiatrists may lead group sessions in which several bipolar patients meet to discuss the pressures of their disorders. That way, patients can learn from each other's successes and failures.

Manic and depressive moods are often triggered by stressful situations. During psychotherapy sessions, patients are encouraged to talk about what may cause stress in their lives. By recognizing stressful situations, bipolar patients can gain an insight into what may be triggering their episodes. Working together, the psychiatrist and patient can develop strategies for confronting or avoiding those stresses. Also, psychiatrists have found that bipolar patients do a better job of staying on their medications when they have regular face-to-face meetings with their therapists.

As part of a patient's treatment regimen, the psychiatrist may recommend cognitive behavioral therapy. This type of therapy was first developed for people who suffer from phobias and other irrational fears. Under cognitive behavioral therapy, patients take small steps toward confronting what frightens them.

Patients who suffer from manic depression can also benefit from cognitive behavioral therapy by learning to recognize the incidents or feelings that can trigger their bipolar episodes. They learn coping strategies, which often include lessons in problem solving. Psychiatrists have found that when patients cannot solve their problems, they often lapse into bipolar episodes. As part of their therapies, patients may be encouraged to keep "mood diaries"—actually writing down events that occur during the day, noting how their moods change during those events. Says James

Maddux, director of clinical psychology at George Mason University in Virginia, "Cognitive therapy teaches the person how to pay attention to his or her thoughts and to try to understand how thoughts influence mood, and helps the person change the way they're thinking to change their mood."[49]

In recent years, psychiatrists have also encouraged family members to become more active in the lives of bipolar patients, emphasizing the importance of maintaining a strong support system at home for the patient. As such, doctors have been working with family members to help them recognize the situations that may trigger manic and depressive moods in their loved ones, and to take steps to eliminate those stresses wherever possible. "It can be something as subtle as a change in a lipstick shade," says Igor Galynker of Beth Israel Medical Center. "Only a person who knows them very, very well would know."[50]

The Bipolar Genes

The best method of treating a bipolar disorder is to recognize it in its earliest form and to control the symptoms before they start dominating the life of a patient. That is why experts in genetics have devoted a lot of their resources to identifying the "bipolar genes." If the genes that trigger bipolar episodes can be definitely identified, it may be possible to develop a test that can identify the bipolar fingerprint in a sample of the patient's hair, saliva, or blood. Armed with that knowledge, doctors and their patients can decide how best to control the symptoms before they develop into severe manic and depressive episodes.

> In their manic phases, bipolar people are often ambitious and super-motivated, which many creative people have turned to their advantage.

Several research projects have developed evidence suggesting some genes are common among all bipolar patients. Still, although there is no question that bipolar disorders are passed down from generation to generation, the science of identifying specific bipolar genes is still inconclusive. In Massachusetts, for example, a joint project by Harvard University and the Massachusetts Institute of Technology has commenced a long-term study to collect tissue samples from bipolar patients. One participant in the study is Francesca Dodd, 67, who has been diagnosed with bipolar disorder. Dodd's mother was also manic depressive.

Dodd knows that a positive identification of the bipolar genes is perhaps years in the future and, therefore, she is not likely to benefit from the science. Still, she says, "I hope it will help the next generation."[51]

Prospering with Bipolar Disorders

Despite having to bear the wild and unpredictable mood swings of bipolar disorders, many patients do go on to live normal and productive lives. Indeed, some very famous and creative people have been diagnosed with bipolar disorders, including many artists, actors, and writers. In their manic phases, bipolar people are often ambitious and super-motivated, which many creative people have turned to their advantage. "It sort of makes intuitive sense," says Galynker. "Some of the things that go into bipolar disorder on the manic side, some of the traits—thinking fast, creativity, charisma, charm—can be very positive."[52]

The list of talented and creative bipolar patients is very long. It includes artist Vincent van Gogh, composer Ludwig van Beethoven, astronaut Buzz Aldrin, actor Robert Downey Jr., British prime minister Winston Churchill, newspaper publisher Philip Graham, author and political activist Abbie Hoffman, and writers Edgar Allan Poe and Mark Twain.

All those people may have accomplished much in their lifetimes, but many also had their dark sides. Van Gogh, Graham, and Hoffman committed suicide. Downey spent time in prison on drug charges before rehabilitating his life and career. Poe died at the age of 40, a day after he was found wandering incoherently in the streets.

Finding the Strength to Cope

Most bipolar patients simply hope to find ways to cope with their disorders and lead normal lives. Mental health professionals know that each bipolar case is different and, therefore, each patient requires a unique blend of drug therapy, psychotherapy, and lifestyle changes to manage his or her symptoms. "Medication has made a big difference in my overall composure, emotional balance, anxiety and sleep difficulty," says Eliza

Richmond, a bipolar patient from Sanford, Maine. "I see my psychiatrist every two months for medication management and psychotherapy. Exercise, diet and breathing exercises are also very important."[53]

Says Brian Marshall, a journalist who lives near Detroit, "After my last major depression, I tried to stay active. I wrote, read, got outside, and tried to stay busy with my family. Also, I underwent therapy twice a week while my medication was being altered."[54]

Most bipolar patients hope to lead lives in which they can work and be productive, enjoy their families, take vacations, and generally get as much out of life as everyone else. And with the proper mood-stabilizing drugs, psychotherapy, and the support of their families, there is no reason they cannot enjoy life to the fullest. Still, most bipolar patients also know that they will always carry the burden of the disorder and that they are constantly living on the edge of depression and mania, and that if they fall over that edge the consequences can be tragic.

Primary Source Quotes*

What Treatments Are Available for Bipolar Disorders?

66 Even though episodes of mania and depression naturally come and go, it is important to understand that bipolar disorder is a long-term illness that currently has no cure. Staying on treatment, even during well times, can help keep the disease under control and reduce the chance of having recurrent, worsening episodes. 99

—National Institute of Mental Health, *Bipolar Disorder*, January 2007. www.nimh.nih.gov.

The National Institute of Mental Health is the federal government's chief funding arm for research into mental illnesses.

....

66 The antidepressants I was given made my moods worse. I'd feel invincible and drive 100 miles an hour or max out my credit cards. Or I'd become very angry, loud and obnoxious: I hadn't experienced outbursts like that before. Friends stopped talking to me, and I was fired from two jobs. 99

—Jennifer Richards, quoted in Stacey Colino, "Cyclothymia: Restoring the Balance," *Saturday Evening Post*, November/December 2006.

Cyclothymia patient Richards works as a receptionist in Boston, Massachusetts.

....

* Editor's Note: While the definition of a primary source can be narrowly or broadly defined, for the purposes of Compact Research, a primary source consists of: 1) results of original research presented by an organization or researcher; 2) eyewitness accounts of events, personal experience, or work experience; 3) first-person editorials offering pundits' opinions; 4) government officials presenting political plans and/or policies; 5) representatives of organizations presenting testimony or policy.

"The fact that antidepressants for bipolar depression were not working or harmful was devastating. Bipolar is difficult to treat. Some think it's treatment-resistant. It's not. But not only do antidepressants not improve bipolar symptoms, they may increase the incidence of mania or cause mixed mania in bipolar individuals."

—Keith Ablow, quoted in Marrecca Fiore, "New Medications More Effective for Treating Bipolar Disorder," Fox News, October 10, 2007. www.foxnews.com.

Ablow is a psychiatrist practicing in Boston, Massachusetts.

"The tragedy is that oftentimes patients will go to their doctors in the depressed phase of the disease, and they will be given antidepressants because it looks like depression. The antidepressants can trigger a manic episode, so medicating patients with bipolar disorder is difficult."

—John D. Port, quoted in Patrick Perry, "New Strategy for Diagnosing Bipolar Disorder," *Saturday Evening Post*, March/April 2005.

Port is an assistant professor of radiology at the Mayo Clinic in Rochester, Minnesota.

"I flirt with not taking [my medications]—but I'm not stupid, because I know every time I've gone off the medication, I've had a breakdown."

—Maurice Benard, quoted in Lauren Cahoon, Radha Chitale, and Aina Hunter, "The Cost of Creativity: Bipolar Disorder and the Stars," ABC News, March 21, 2008. http://abcnews.go.com.

Benard, who is bipolar, is a member of the cast of the daytime drama *General Hospital*.

❝I make sure I take all my medications, get enough sleep, and eat enough food. . . . I'm also careful to keep my work life in perspective. I have lost more jobs than I can count because of crying at work. I also take care of my body, mind and soul.❞

—Kelly Barratt, quoted in Michelle Roberts, "The Many Faces and Facets of BP," *BP*, Summer 2007. www.bphope.com.

Barratt, a bipolar patient, works as a corporate financial analyst in Austin, Texas.

❝The treatment that helped the most has been medication. I do go to counseling, but it is hard to get anywhere with therapy until the mood swings are more under control.❞

— Laurel Powell, quoted in Michelle Roberts, "The Many Faces and Facets of BP," *BP*, Summer 2007. www.bphope.com.

Powell, a bipolar patient, is a massage therapist who lives in Medford, Oregon.

❝Keeping some kind of mood diary is an excellent way of learning how to get better control of one's moods. The whole point of the exercise is to try to find a pattern . . . and see what is triggering bad and good moods.❞

—James Maddux, quoted in Shelley Widhalm, "Moods: Up, Down, Gray," *Washington Times*, August 29, 2006.

Maddux is director of clinical psychology at George Mason University in Virginia.

❝Someday it may be possible to reliably assess risk for psychiatric disorders. But at this point, the technology—and the science—is still evolving.❞

—Michael Miller, quoted in Faye Flam, "Harvard Researchers Skeptical of Commercial Genetics Test," *Philadelphia Inquirer*, May 12, 2008.

Miller is editor of the *Harvard Mental Health Letter*.

❝I'm not so much smarter than other people as faster. I swing more often, I make errors, but I make them faster. That's how I sometimes describe it. If you can focus this energy, you can do great things with it. If not, well, I think it can be difficult.❞

—Laurence McKinney, quoted in Benedict Carey, "Hypomanic? Absolutely. But Oh So Productive!" *New York Times*, March 22, 2005.

McKinney, a hypomania patient, is a business consultant from Boston.

....

❝That is one of the most difficult things of treating bipolar disorder. If someone is fantastically creative do you want to make them just averagely creative?❞

—Igor Galynker, quoted in Lauren Cahoon, Radha Chitale, and Aina Hunter, "The Cost of Creativity: Bipolar Disorder and the Stars," ABC News, March 21, 2008. http://abcnews.go.com.

Galynker is director of the Family Center for Bipolar Disorder at Beth Israel Medical Center in New York.

....

❝When I've come down from these terribly entertaining and insightful manias, I've found myself with things like 1,400 pages of garbage, or entire manuscripts of totally impenetrable, highly alliterative 'poetry' that is almost awe-inspiringly bad.❞

—Marya Hornbacher, quoted in "An Interview with Marya Hornbacher: On the Forthcoming Memoir *Madness: A Bipolar Life*," 2008. www.maryahornbacher.com.

Hornbacher, a bipolar patient, is the author of the memoir *Madness: A Bipolar Life*.

....

What Treatments Are Available for Bipolar Disorders?

- Lithium by itself is effective in about **50 percent** of bipolar patients.

- A California study found that bipolar patients who do not take lithium are **three times more likely to commit suicide** than bipolar patients who take the drug.

- **Fifty-five percent** of bipolar patients who take lithium begin to develop a resistance to the drug within three years, meaning their doctors either have to increase their doses or supplement the drug with other medications.

- An Italian study found that just **29 percent** of bipolar patients who took lithium experienced a total remission in their symptoms.

- Group therapy improves by **86 percent** the chances that bipolar patients will stay on their medications and conform to other therapies.

- **One in four** bipolar patients is correctly diagnosed within the first three years of exhibiting symptoms.

- **Ninety percent** of bipolar patients say they are satisfied with the effectiveness of their medications.

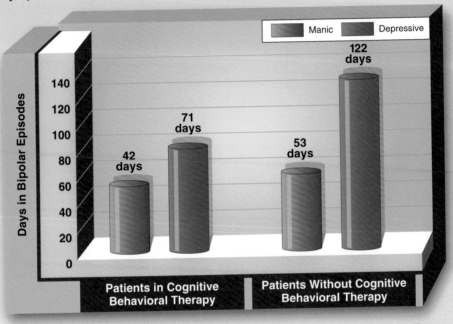

Effectiveness of Cognitive Behavioral Therapy on Bipolar Patients

In cognitive behavioral therapy, or CBT, bipolar patients work with their psychotherapists to learn to recognize or deal with the stressful events in their lives that may trigger their manic and depressive symptoms. A study by the Institute of Psychology at King's College London in Great Britain followed 95 bipolar patients who were enrolled in cognitive behavioral therapy as well as 201 bipolar patients in a control group who did not participate in CBT. The results indicate that the CBT patients spent fewer days in the throes of their manic and depressive symptoms than the patients in the group without CBT.

Source: Dominic H. Lam et al., "Relapse Prevention in Patients with Bipolar Disorder: Cognitive Therapy Outcome After 2 Years," *American Journal of Psychiatry*, February 2005.

- According to a Pennsylvania study, bipolar teenagers who take the drug **valproate**, which is used to reduce seizures in epileptic patients, cut their alcohol abuse to half that of bipolar teenagers who were given a placebo.

Side Effects of Lithium in Rapid Cyclers

Lithium, which is the most widely prescribed drug for bipolar disorders, can cause a number of unpleasant side effects in patients, particularly in rapid cyclers. A study by Case Western Reserve Hospital in Cleveland, Ohio, identified stomachaches, tremors, and frequent urination as the most common side effects among 32 patients who participated in the study.

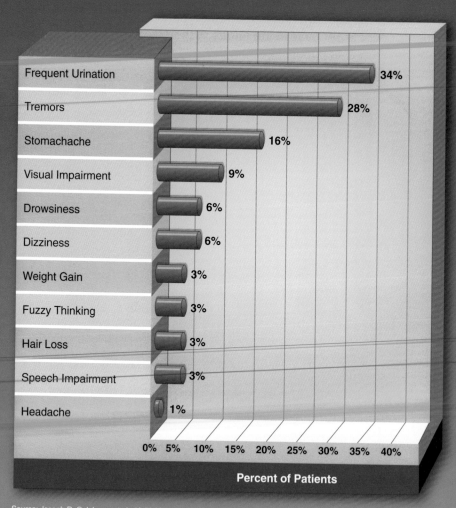

Source: Joseph R. Calabrese et al., "A 20-Month, Double-Blind, Maintenance Trial of Lithium Versus Divalproex in Rapid-Cycling Bipolar Disorder," *American Journal of Psychiatry*, November 2005.

- **Sixty percent** of bipolar patients who live alone or otherwise do not have the support of their families are likely to be hospitalized, while just **12 percent** of patients with strong family support are likely to spend time in the hospital.

Intensive Psychotherapy Aids in Recovery

A University of Colorado study found that bipolar patients suffering from depression recovered faster if they received intensive psycho-therapy rather than occasional visits to their psychiatrists. During the year-long study 163 patients in the "intensive group" saw their psychiatrists 30 times in a 9-month span while 130 patients in the "collaborative group" saw their psychiatrists 3 times in 6 weeks. For the intensive patients, the average time of recovery was 110 days faster than the collaborative patients. Also, a higher percentage of intensive psychotherapy patients made full recoveries from their depressive symptoms—64 percent as opposed to 52 percent of the collaborative psychotherapy patients.

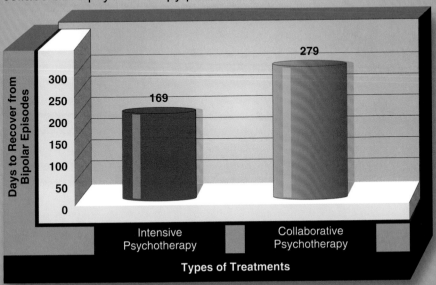

Source: National Institute of Mental Health, "Intensive Psychotherapy More Effective than Brief Therapy for Treating Bipolar Depression," April 2, 2007. www.nimh.nih.gov.

Family Therapy Effective Among Young Bipolar Patients

In a study by the universities of Colorado and Pittsburgh, 30 teenage bipolar patients were provided with intensive family-focused therapy over a period of 9 months, while 28 teenage patients were provided with enhanced care, which included 3 sessions in which they were schooled on how to take their medications, how to avoid conflicts, and how to prepare for relapses. Over the course of the study, the average patient receiving family-focused therapy recovered from depressive symptoms a month sooner than the average enhanced-care patient.

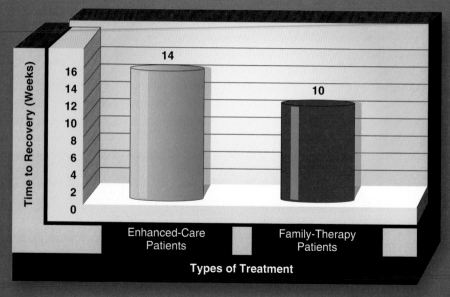

Source: National Institute of Mental Health, "Family Focused Therapy Effective in Treating Depressive Episodes of Bipolar Youth," September 1, 2008. www.nimh.nih.gov.

- As many as **52 percent** of bipolar patients neglect to take their medications as prescribed.

- Lithium is ineffective in up to **82 percent** of bipolar patients who experience frequent episodes of rapid cycling.

Key People and Advocacy Groups

American Psychiatric Association: Publisher of the *Diagnostic and Statistical Manual of Mental Disorders*, the American Psychiatric Association guides the country's 38,000 psychiatrists on how to treat mental illnesses, including bipolar disorders. In 1980 the *DSM* changed the name of the illness from manic depression to bipolar disorder, and in 1994 an updated version of the *DSM* split bipolar disorders into three main categories.

Beth Israel Medical Center Family Center for Bipolar Disorder: The New York–based hospital has made family-focused therapy a priority in the treatment of bipolar patients. In family-focused therapy, spouses and children of bipolar patients learn how to eliminate the stresses and other triggers that prompt manic and depressive symptoms in their loved ones.

John Cade: The Australian psychiatrist discovered that lithium could control the symptoms of manic depression. Since Cade first administered lithium to patients in 1948, the drug has been established as the most effective treatment for bipolar disorders, although doctors frequently supplement it with other drugs. Cade served as president of the Australian and New Zealand College of Psychiatrists and, for his discovery, was named a distinguished fellow of the American Psychiatric Association. He died in 1980.

Terri Cheney, Marya Hornbacher, Autumn Stringam, and Jane Pauley: Cheney, Hornbacher, Stringam, and Pauley are bipolar patients who have authored memoirs in recent years recounting their struggles with manic depression. Cheney is an attorney, Hornbacher is a writer and novelist, Pauley is a TV journalist, and Stringam is a Canadian mother of four.

Jules Falret: The French psychiatrist published a paper noting the symptoms of bipolar disorder in 1854, calling the illness *folie circulaire*, which means "circular insanity." Falret's description of the illness and its symptoms was challenged by another French psychiatrist, Jules Baillarger, who also issued a paper on the illness and claimed to have been the first to diagnose the symptoms in his patients. However, Falret's paper was published a week before Baillarger's paper, enabling Falret to take the credit.

Harvard University and the Massachusetts Institute of Technology: The two universities are conducting a joint project to collect tissue samples from bipolar patients. By analyzing thousands of samples, scientists at Harvard and MIT hope to find genes that are common among all bipolar patients.

Institute of Psychiatry, King's College London: King's College London's Institute of Psychiatry launched the Maudsley Bipolar Twin Study in 2003, hoping to establish genetic and environmental roots in bipolar disorders. More than 80 pairs of twins—including bipolar and nonbipolar patients—have provided tissue samples, which contain their DNA. They have also taken tests demonstrating their neurological abilities and have undergone magnetic resonance imaging scans of their brains.

Margot Kidder, Carrie Fisher, and Linda Hamilton: The three actresses rose to fame as action film stars—Kidder as Lois Lane in the *Superman* movies, Fisher as Princess Leia in the *Star Wars* films, and Hamilton as Sarah Connor in the *Terminator* movies. All three abused drugs and alcohol while enduring symptoms of bipolar disorder. Kidder, Fisher, and Hamilton have shaken off their drug and alcohol addictions and have gained control of their bipolar symptoms. The three actresses speak openly about their struggles, urging others not to follow their examples.

Emil Kraepelin: The German psychiatrist first used the term *manic depression* to describe the illness in an 1896 psychiatric textbook that he authored. He noted the course of the illness in patients, finding that periods of depression were followed by periods of mania.

Demitri Papolos and Janice Papolos: Psychiatrist Demitri Papolos and his wife, Janice, are coauthors of the 1999 book *The Bipolar Child*, in which they suggest that at least a million bipolar children have been misdiagnosed with attention deficit hyperactive disorder. The book helped prove that it is possible for very young children to develop bipolar symptoms, a notion that had been rejected by psychiatrists for decades.

Chronology

1899
Wilhelm Weygandt, a German psychiatrist, suggests that mixed mania episodes are possible in manic depression; he also describes the symptoms of hypomania.

About 2500 B.C.
Greek physician Hippocrates first notes the symptoms of bipolar disorders in patients, calling the illness "mania and melancholia."

1966
Psychiatrists Jules Angst of Switzerland and Carlo Perris of Sweden conclude that bipolar disorder and depression are separate mood disorders; Angst and Perris are also the first physicians to use the term *bipolar* in describing the illness.

1896
German psychiatrist Emil Kraepelin first uses the term *manic depression* in his book on the disorder; he also notes an increased number of manic episodes in bipolar women shortly after they give birth.

1800   **1900**   **1965**   **1970**

A.D. 1817
Swedish chemist Johann August Arfvedson discovers a new element—a soft metal he names lithium, after the Greek word *lithos*, which means "stone."

1882
The term *cyclothymia* is first used by German psychiatrist Karl Kahlbaum, who describes the symptoms of the disorder.

1967
Iconic rock guitarist Jimi Hendrix releases the album *Are You Experienced*, featuring the single "Manic Depression." Although there is no evidence that Hendrix was bipolar, he led a decidedly unpredictable life and died of a drug overdose in 1970.

1854
French physician Jules Falret defines the symptoms of the illness, labeling it *folie circulaire*, which means "circular insanity." Falret also correctly deduces that the disorder is passed from generation to generation.

1948
Australian psychiatrist John Cade finds that chemical salts extracted from the element lithium have a calming effect on laboratory animals and soon administers the drug to manic depressive patients.

1970
The U.S. Food and Drug Administration approves the use of lithium to treat manic depression patients in America.

1972

Missouri senator Thomas Eagleton, the Democratic candidate for vice president, is forced to withdraw from the ticket after newspapers report he underwent electroconvulsive therapy for an unnamed mental illness. Later, Eagleton's running mate, presidential candidate George McGovern, discloses that Eagleton suffered from a bipolar disorder.

1985

The Chicago, Illinois–based Depression and Bipolar Support Alliance is founded, becoming one of the largest national organizations to provide support to bipolar patients.

1999

Psychiatrist Demitri Papolos and his wife, Janice, publish the book *The Bipolar Child*, in which they suggest that at least a million bipolar children have been misdiagnosed with attention deficit hyperactive disorder.

1994

The American Psychiatric Association designates three main categories of the illness, bipolar I, bipolar II with hypomania, and cyclothymic disorder. A fourth category, bipolar disorder not otherwise specified, is also designated.

1970   **1985**   **2000**

1988

Academy Award–winning actress Patty Duke publishers her autobiography, *Call Me Anna*, in which she describes her life with bipolar disorder. Duke's book is one of the first by a celebrity to acknowledge the affliction.

1995

A study by Massachusetts General Hospital first raises the notion that bipolar disorders are a lot more common in children than psychiatrists previously believed.

1980

The American Psychiatric Association officially changes the name of the illness from manic depression to bipolar disorder.

2004

Physicians at the Mayo Clinic in Rochester, Minnesota, report the first results of brain-scanning experiments in which they employed magnetic resonance imaging techniques to produce evidence of bipolar disorder in patients.

2007

Bipolar Disorder, a publication issued by the National Institute of Mental Health, estimates the number of bipolar patients in America over the age of 18 at 5.7 million, or about 2.6 percent of the adult population.

Related Organizations

American Psychological Association (APA)

750 First St. NE

Washington, DC 20002-4242

phone: (800) 374-2721

Web site: www.apa.org • e-mail: public.affairs@apa.org

The American Psychological Association represents more than 148,000 American psychologists, who are professionals who study and treat human behavior. Visitors to the association's Web site can access current and past issues of APA's magazine, *Monitor on Psychology*, which has published many articles about bipolar disorders.

Association for Behavioral and Cognitive Therapies

305 Seventh Ave., 16th Floor

New York, NY 10001

phone: (212) 647-1890 • fax: (212) 647-1865

Web site: www.aabt.org

The association represents therapists who provide cognitive behavioral therapy for people who suffer from many types of mental illnesses, including mood disorders. Students who visit the association's Web site can find fact sheets on a long list of mental illnesses that may be treated by cognitive behavioral therapy, including bipolar disorders.

Child and Adolescent Bipolar Foundation

1000 Skokie Blvd., Suite 570

Wilmette, IL 60091

phone: (847) 256-8525 • fax: (847) 920-9498

Web site: www.bpkids.org

Founded in 1999, the Child and Adolescent Bipolar Foundation provides support to the parents of children and teens who have been diagnosed with bipolar disorders. Visitors to the association's Web site can find a background on bipolar disorders, a chronology of important dates in the history of the illness, advice on how to find a doctor, and updates on research projects that focus on bipolar disorders.

Depression and Bipolar Support Alliance

730 N. Franklin St., Suite 501

Chicago, IL 60654-7225

phone: (800) 826-3632 • fax: (312) 642-7243

Web site: www.dbsalliance.org • e-mail: info@dbsalliance.org

The Depression and Bipolar Support Alliance has established more than 400 community-based chapters that provide support for mood disorder patients and their families. The alliance also provides educational materials to schools, the media, and other interested groups, and lobbies in Washington for laws that support mental health education and research.

International Society for Bipolar Disorders

PO Box 7168

Pittsburgh, PA 15213-0168

phone: (412) 802-6940 • fax: (412) 802-6941

Web site: www.isbd.org

The society coordinates efforts among bipolar support and research groups in the United States and other countries. Visitors to the organization's Web site can find a background on the illness and links to Web sites for several international mental health agencies.

Juvenile Bipolar Research Foundation

550 Ridgewood Rd.

Maplewood, NJ 07040

phone: (866) 333-5273 • fax: (973) 275-0420

Web site: www.jbrf.org • e-mail: info@jbrf.org

The Juvenile Bipolar Research Foundation raises money to support scientific research that focuses on helping children overcome bipolar disorders. Visitors to the organization's Web site can receive updates on the research projects the foundation has funded; parents of bipolar children can obtain information on whether their children qualify to be included in the studies.

Massachusetts General Hospital Bipolar Clinic and Research Program

50 Staniford St., Suite 580

Boston, MA 02114

phone: (617) 726-6188

Web site: www.manicdepressive.org

Some of the most important research into bipolar disorders is conducted at the Massachusetts General Hospital Bipolar Clinic and Research Program. Typically, the clinic maintains about 10 ongoing research projects delving into the causes, treatments, and symptoms of bipolar disorder. Visitors to the clinic's Web site can find brief descriptions of the clinic's research projects as well as answers to some basic questions about bipolar disorders.

Mental Health America

2000 N. Beauregard St., 6th Floor

Alexandria, VA 22311

phone: (800) 969-6642 • fax: (703) 684-5968

Web site: www.nmha.org

Formerly the National Mental Health Association, Mental Health America is an advocacy group for people with mental illnesses as well as for their families. Students can find many resources on the organization's Web site about bipolar disorders, including fact sheets on such complications as alcohol and drug abuse, physical ailments, and changes in personality often suffered by bipolar patients.

National Alliance on Mental Illness

Colonial Place Three

2107 Wilson Blvd., Suite 300

Arlington, VA 22201-3042

phone: (703) 524-7600 • fax: (703) 524-9094

Web site: www.nami.org

The alliance is an advocacy group for people with mental illnesses and includes local chapters in every state. The organization's Web site provides access to articles published in *BP* magazine, which features many interviews with bipolar patients and other stories about coping with the disease.

National Institute of Mental Health

6001 Executive Blvd.

Bethesda, MD 20892-9663

phone: (866) 615-6464

Web site: www.nimh.nih.gov • e-mail: nimhinfo@nih.gov

An agency of the National Institutes of Health, the National Institute of Mental Health is the federal government's chief funding agency for mental health research in America. The 2007 publication *Bipolar Disorders*, which provides an overview of the illness, can be downloaded from the agency's Web site.

For Further Research

Books
Tracy Anglada, *Intense Minds: Through the Eyes of Young People with Bipolar Disorder*. Victoria, BC: Trafford, 2006.

Wes Burgess, *The Bipolar Handbook*. New York: Avery, 2006.

Terri Cheney, *Manic: A Memoir*. New York: William Morrow, 2008.

Virginia Edwards, *Depression and Bipolar Disorders*. Buffalo, NY: Firefly, 2002.

Jan Fawcett, Bernard Golden, and Nancy Rosenfeld, *New Hope for People with Bipolar Disorder*. New York: Three Rivers, 2007.

Marya Hornbacher, *Madness: A Bipolar Life*. Boston: Houghton Mifflin, 2008.

Emily Martin, *Bipolar Expeditions: Mania and Depression in American Culture*. Princeton, NJ: Princeton University Press, 2007.

Francis Mark Mondimore, *Bipolar: A Guide for Patients and Families*. Baltimore: Johns Hopkins University Press, 2004.

Jane Pauley, *Skywriting: A Life Out of the Blue*. New York: Random House, 2004.

Autumn Stringam, *A Promise of Hope*. Toronto: HarperCollins Canada, 2007.

Periodicals
Nicholas Bakalar, "Long-Term Therapy Effective in Bipolar Depression," *New York Times*, April 10, 2007.

Carole Braden, "A Dark Secret," *Good Housekeeping*, January 2005.

Benedict Carey, "Hypomanic? Absolutely. But Oh So Productive!" *New York Times*, March 22, 2005.

Mary Carmichael, "Welcome to Max's World," *Newsweek*, May 26, 2008.

Terri Cheney, "Take Me as I Am, Whoever I Am," *New York Times*, January 13, 2008.

Andy Coghlan, "Young and Moody or Mentally Ill?" *New Scientist*, May 19, 2007.

Stacey Colino, "Cyclothymia: Restoring the Balance," *Saturday Evening Post*, November/December 2006.

Gareth Cook, "Geneticists Map What Makes Us Different," *Boston Globe*, October 27, 2005.

Jerome Goopman, "What's Normal?" *New Yorker*, April 9, 2007.

Anemona Hartocollis, "Clinic Treats Mental Illness by Enlisting the Family," *New York Times*, June 4, 2008.

Joe Joseph, "Manic Depression Touches Fry's Soul," *Times* (London), September 20, 2006.

Jeffrey Kluger et al., "Young and Bipolar," *Time*, August 19, 2002.

Patrick Perry, "New Strategy for Diagnosing Bipolar Disorder," *Saturday Evening Post*, March/April 2005.

——, "Jane Pauley: Tackling the Stigma of Bipolar Disorder," *Saturday Evening Post*, March/April 2007.

Sandy Fertman Ryan, "Stranger in My House," *Girls' Life*, February 2006.

Joe Saraceno, "A Troubled Life on the Line," *USA Today*, February 3, 2005.

Saturday Evening Post, "Mood Swings: An Interview with Peter Whybrow," July/August 2005.

David M. Shribman, "Black Moods in the White House: Many Presidents Suffered from Mental Illness and Yet They Were Highly Functional and Successful," *Pittsburgh Post-Gazette*, May 21, 2006.

Autumn Stringam, "My New Ordinary Life," *Chatelaine*, May 2008.

Shelley Widhalm, "Moods: Up, Down, Gray," *Washington Times*, August 29, 2006.

Internet Sources

Lauren Cahoon, Radha Chitale, and Aina Hunter, "The Cost of Creativity: Bipolar Disorder and the Stars," ABC News, March 21, 2008. http://abcnews.go.com/Health/MindMoodNews/Story?id=44390 15&page=2.

Mayo Clinic, "Bipolar Disorder." www.mayoclinic.com/health/bipolar-disorder/DS00356.

National Institute of Mental Health, *Bipolar Disorder*. www.nimh.nih. gov/health/topics/bipolar-disorder/index.shtml.

Michelle Roberts, "The Many Faces and Facets of BP," *BP*, Summer 2007. www.bphope.com/Item.aspx?id=64.

U.S. Substance Abuse and Mental Health Services Administration, "Mood Disorders." http://mentalhealth.samhsa.gov/publications/all pubs/ken98-0049/default.asp.

Source Notes

Overview

1. Quoted in Joe Joseph, "Manic Depression Touches Fry's Soul," *Times* (London), September 20, 2006, p. 27.

2. Quoted in Joe Saraceno, "A Troubled Life on the Line," *USA Today*, February 3, 2005, p. 1-Sports.

3. Quoted in Nancy Gay, "Wife Says Robbins Has Lost Will to Live," *San Francisco Chronicle*, January 26, 2005, p. D-2.

4. Quoted in Andreas Mameros and Frederick K. Goodwin, eds., *Bipolar Disorders: Mixed States, Rapid Cycling and Atypical Forms*. Cambridge: Cambridge University Press, 2005, p. 5.

5. Wes Burgess, *The Bipolar Handbook*. New York: Avery, 2006, p. 10.

6. Quoted in Mary Carmichael, "Welcome to Max's World," *Newsweek*, May 26, 2008, p. 32.

7. Quoted in Jerome Goopman, "What's Normal?" *New Yorker*, April 9, 2007, p. 28.

8. Quoted in Jane Glenn Haas, "Author Trains Spotlight on Bipolar Disorder," *Orange County (CA) Register*, February 26, 2008. www.ocregister.com.

9. Quoted in Haas, "Author Trains Spotlight on Bipolar Disorder."

10. Quoted in John E. Mulligan, "The Healing of Patrick J. Kennedy," *BP*, Spring 2007. www.bphope.com.

11. Quoted in *Science Daily*, "Anticonvulsant Drug Cuts Drinking in Bipolar Alcoholics, Shows University of Pittsburgh Research," January 19, 2005. www.sciencedaily.com.

12. Quoted in Carole Braden, "A Dark Secret," *Good Housekeeping*, January 2005, p. 119.

13. Quoted in Anemona Hartocollis, "Clinic Treats Mental Illness by Enlisting the Family," *New York Times*, June 4, 2008, p. B-1.

What Are Bipolar Disorders and What Are the Symptoms?

14. Marya Hornbacher, *Madness: A Bipolar Life*. Boston: Houghton Mifflin, 2008, p. 20.

15. Quoted in Sara Solovitch, "People Like Me," *BP*, Summer 2006. www.bphope.com.

16. Quoted in Jan Fawcett, Bernard Golden, and Nancy Rosenfeld, *New Hope for People with Bipolar Disorder*. New York: Three Rivers, 2007, p. 6.

17. Quoted in Fawcett, Golden, and Rosenfeld, *New Hope for People with Bipolar Disorder*, p. 12.

18. Quoted in Michelle Roberts, "The Many Faces and Facets of BP," *BP*, Summer 2007. www.bphope.com.

19. Quoted in *Saturday Evening Post*, "An Excerpt from *Skywriting: A Life Out of the Blue*," March/April 2007, p. 53.

20. Quoted in *Saturday Evening Post*, "An Excerpt from *Skywriting*," p. 53.

21. Quoted in Stacey Colino, "Cyclothymia: Restoring the Balance," *Saturday Evening Post*, November/December 2006, p. 91.

22. Quoted in Colino, "Cyclothymia," p. 91.

23. Hornbacher, *Madness*, p. 146.

What Causes Bipolar Disorders?

24. Quoted in *Saturday Evening Post*, "Mood Swings: An Interview with Peter Whybrow," July/August 2005, p. 36.

25. David J. Milkowitz and Elizabeth L. George, *The Bipolar Teen*. New York: Guilford, 2008, p. 123.

26. Quoted in *Women's Health Weekly*, "Mental Health, Hormonal Changes and Depression: What Is the Connection?" November 29, 2007, p. 242.

27. Quoted in Michelle Roberts, "When Conception Is the Question," *BP*, Spring 2007. www.bphope.com.

28. Quoted in Roberts, "When Conception Is the Question."

29. Quoted in Colino, "Cyclothymia," p. 91.

30. Marianne Z. Wamboldt and David Reiss, "Explorations of Parenting Environments in the Evolution of Psychiatric Problems in Children," *American Journal of Psychiatry*, June 2006, p. 951.

31. Quoted in Dan Vergano, "What Makes Circadian Rhythms Tick?" *USA Today*, June 19, 2007. www.usatoday.com.

32. Quoted in BBC News Channel, "Bipolar Disorder 'Shrinks Brain,'" July 20, 2007. http://news.bbc.co.uk.

How Do Bipolar Disorders Affect People?

33. Fawcett, Golden, and Rosenfeld, *New Hope for People with Bipolar Disorder*, p. 23.

34. Quoted in Sandy Fertman Ryan, "Stranger in My House," *Girls' Life*, February 2006, p. 64.

35. Quoted in Fertman Ryan, "Stranger in My House," p. 64.

36. Terri Cheney, *Manic: A Memoir*. New York: William Morrow, 2008, p. 155.

37. Quoted in Lauren Cahoon, Radha Chitale, and Aina Hunter, "The Cost of Creativity: Bipolar Disorder and the Stars," ABC News, March 21, 2008. http://abcnews.go.com.

38. Quoted in Patricia McAdams, "Mood Matters," *Lancaster (PA) New Era*, August 22, 2005, p. 1.

39. Hornbacher, *Madness*, p. 271.

40. Quoted in John Anderson, "Soap Star Maurice Benard: The Rebel Has a Cause," fall 2007. *BP*. www.bphope.com.

41. Terri Cheney, "Take Me as I Am, Whoever I Am," *New York Times*, January 13, 2008, section 9–6.

42. Quoted in Greg Griffin, "Webroot Founder's Tragic Turn Mystifying," *Denver Post*, July 17, 2008. www.denverpost.com.

What Treatments Are Available for Bipolar Disorders?

43. Burgess, *The Bipolar Handbook*, p. 4.

44. Quoted in Patrick Perry, "New Strategy for Diagnosing Bipolar Disorder," *Saturday Evening Post*, March/April 2005, p. 64.

45. Quoted in Patrick Perry, "Bipolar Disorder: On the Brink of Discovery," *Saturday Evening Post*, January/February 2007, p. 78.

46. Quoted in Marrecca Fiore, "New Medications More Effective for Treating Bipolar Disorder," Fox News, October 10, 2007. www.foxnews.com.

47. Quoted in Cahoon, Chitale, and Hunter, "The Cost of Creativity."

48. Quoted in Sara Solovitch, "ECT: When All Else Fails," *BP*, Winter 2006. www.

bphope.com.

49. Quoted in Shelley Widhalm, "Moods: Up, Down, Gray," *Washington Times*, August 29, 2006, p. B-4.

50. Quoted in Hartocollis, "Clinic Treats Mental Illness by Enlisting the Family," p. B-1.

51. Quoted in Gareth Cook, "Geneticists Map What Makes Us Different," *Boston Globe*, October 27, 2005, p. A-1.

52. Quoted in Cahoon, Chitale, and Hunter, "The Cost of Creativity."

53. Quoted in Roberts, "The Many Faces and Facets of BP."

54. Quoted in Roberts, "The Many Faces and Facets of BP."

List of Illustrations

Index

About the Author

Hal Marcovitz, a writer based in Chalfont, Pennsylvania, has written more than 100 books for young readers. His other titles in the Compact Research series include *Phobias*, *Hepatitis*, and *Meningitis*.